Also by Laurie Beth Jones

*Jesus, CEO: Using Ancient Wisdom
for Visionary Leadership*
*Jesus in Blue Jeans: A Practical Guide to
Everyday Spirituality*
*The Power of Positive Prophecy:
Finding the Hidden Potential in Everyday Life*

—THE—
PATH

HYPERION
New York

THE
PATH

Creating Your Mission
Statement for Work and
for Life

Laurie Beth Jones

Library of Congress Cataloging-in-Publication Data

Jones, Laurie Beth.
    The Path : creating your mission statement for
work and for life / Laurie Beth Jones. — 1st ed.
        p.   cm.
    ISBN 0-7868-6227-0
        1. Vocation.   2. Mission Statements.
    I. Title.
BV4740.J66   1996
248.4 — DC20   6-846
                                                    CIP

PAPERBACK ISBN 0-7868-8241-7

BOOK DESIGN BY CLAUDYNE BIANCO BEDELL

FIRST PAPERBACK EDITION

10   9

To all those who truly seek
The Path
and then follow it
with courage.

Contents

Introduction   ix

I. FINDING YOUR MISSION   1

Three Elements of a Good Mission Statement   3

Eleven False Assumptions about Missions   9

Forming a Sense of Mission   23

Who Are You?   33

    Personalities with a Past   33

    The Power of Positive Prophecy   38

    Finding Your USP   41

    Looking at Your Gifts—Today   44

Your Passion Is Your Power   49

Creating the Vision Statement   71

Sustaining Creative Tension   93

II. FULFILLING YOUR MISSION 101

The Eight Action Steps to Succes   103

Case Studies   115

   Nehemiah   115

   Joan of Arc   131

   Queen Esther   140

   Joseph   149

   Moses   155

   Ruth   161

Pitfalls and Potholes   169

III. CASE HISTORY: PERSONAL 211

IV. MEDITATIONS 227

Conclusion 231

Acknowledgments 233

Gift Offer 235

Index 237

Introduction

My uncle once told me that during World War II if an unidentified soldier appeared suddenly in the dark and could not state his mission, he was automatically shot without question. I wonder what would happen if we reinstituted that policy today.

Being confronted with a "life or death" need to know one's mission would force millions of us to reexamine who we are, and what we're really about. It would save immeasurable amounts of money, tears, and heartache. Absenteeism would drop. Productivity would soar. Leaders of Congress, corporations, institutions, and associations would be forced to exchange rhetoric for real and meaningful action. People who linger in the shadows, leading unfulfilled lives, would burst into the sunlight of

Possibilities and Power. Those who have never known what it's like to feel a passionate commitment to a cause would be catapulted from their couches onto the playing field, tasting the dirt, feeling the sweat and the sting of tears and having the wind knocked out of them . . . and in the process become fully alive.

Those who have never breathed deep the lilac smell of victory or felt the tingling thrill that comes from having accomplished a mighty task would suddenly know, deep down in their bones, that they came here with a purpose far greater than "to survive."

In the book *Repacking Your Bags*, authors Richard Leider and David Shapiro state that their research shows that the number one deadly fear of people is "Having lived a meaningless life." Finding one's mission, and then fulfilling it, is perhaps the most vital activity in which a person can engage.

Recent best-selling books like Stephen Covey's *Putting First Things First* and the seminal business book *Reengineering the Corporation* by Michael Hammer and James Champy stress the importance of individuals and corporations developing mission statements. A mission statement is, in essence, a written-down reason for being— whether for a person, or for a company. It is the key to finding your path in life and identifying the mission you choose to follow. Having a clearly articulated mission statement gives one a template of purpose that can be used to initiate, evaluate, and refine all of one's activities.

While mission statements seem only recently to have sprung into the public consciousness, they have, in fact, been around for centuries. One of the most powerful and influential leaders of all time articulated his mission statement in a single sentence two thousand years ago: "I came that they might have life, and have it more abundantly." Every activity that he undertook—whether turning water into wine, playing with children, holding seminars by the sea, or challenging the current religious system—was a result of his mission statement. That statement covered not only his work life, but also his personal and leisure time, as well. It also helped him determine and focus his activities. When the woman caught in adultery was brought before him, he refused to judge her, saying again, "My mission is not to condemn, but to give life." Knowing his mission helped him decide how to act, what to do, and even what to say when challenging situations arose.

Webster's College Dictionary (Random House) gives several definitions of the word "mission." Among them are:

—— a specific task that a person or group of persons is sent to perform;

— the place of work of such persons, or the
territory of their responsibility;

— military operational task, usually
assigned by a higher headquarters;

— an aerospace operation designed to carry
out the goals of a specific program;

— an allotted or self-imposed duty or task;
calling.

It doesn't take more than a quick read through the morning
newspapers or a casual walk through a corporate cafeteria to
realize that many people are not following or do not have a
"mission" as Webster's defines one. There is rampant confusion and misunderstanding about the specificity and importance of the tasks each one is called to do. Unemployment,
absenteeism, and labor problems all attest to this fact.
Governments as well as companies and individuals are strug-
gling almost daily to define exactly what their "territory of
responsibility" is. Too much of what is going on in the world
has not, in fact, been assigned by a "higher headquarters,"
but is merely a reflection of the human ego left unchecked.

A recent piece on *60 Minutes* highlighted the plight
of thousands of workers who have been caught in the
"down" part of downsizing. An overwhelming number of
them are mid- to upper-level managers, most are slightly

over fifty years of age, and many of them have more than twenty years worth of work experience. The road to re-employment has been strewn with the casualties of divorce, despair, and ever sagging self-esteem. These are people who were playing by the rules and even winning the game—until the game changed. I was saddened after seeing the show—it all seemed so overwhelming and hopeless.

But that is all the more reason that the case studies I've selected to profile in *The Path* are pertinent today. Of the six people I profile, three had to create new jobs for themselves after their old jobs no longer seemed relevant. Four of them found themselves in life-threatening situations as a result of sudden power shifts from the top, and nearly all of them had to relocate. Without exception, each of them had to learn new skills as their world turned upside down.

Yet, they survived. So will we. And, in spite of all their hardships, they emerged victorious—with legendary exploits to share from their missions. So can we.

While so much attention has been paid to the downsizing of America, not enough attention has been paid to the "wrongsizing" of America. In a study conducted by *Fortune* magazine, nearly 50 percent of all women executives had recently thought about or were currently thinking about leaving their jobs. Having shattered the glass ceiling and climbed the corporate ladder, many found it was, for them, leaning against the wrong wall.

At a meeting in San Francisco a gasp went round the room when the leader announced that the president of American Express corporation had just quit his $4-million-dollar-a-year job. He left because, in his words, he was looking "for a life." Statistics underscore the frustrations of workers—even at the top. The average lifespan of a corporate CEO is four years. Hospital administrators last three to five years. Where do these people go when their jobs are no longer enough?

Recently I received a letter from a veterinarian in the Northwest who wanted a consulting appointment so that I could help her sort out her true talents. Being gifted and trained in the area of helping animals, she now found herself being called to lead and motivate people. "Is there a conflict?" she wanted to know. Could I—or anybody else—help her, and "how soon?"

Her cry has been echoed by many. Perhaps she doesn't need a new job, but a broader definition of her mission statement. She needs a mission that will encompass and utilize not only her trained professional skills but also her innate gifts and abilities as well.

Having worked for the last ten years assisting individuals and groups in writing mission statements, I know firsthand what an arduous process it is. One group I observed took three painful years to complete one. Stephen Covey recently revealed that it took his family eight months to complete theirs. Corporations have costly retreats and spend literally hundreds of thousands of dollars hiring consultants to help them with the process. Individuals seek out career counselors, and take expensive and lengthy tests to determine their strengths and weaknesses—all in an attempt to help them define a purpose and direction for their life.

As I have traveled the country, doing book tours and seminars on the topic of *Jesus, CEO,* I have encountered many confused and unfulfilled workers. In these seminars, the topic "Finding Your Mission," which was originally scheduled for one hour, evolved into its own full-fledged three-day workshop.

As I consulted with individuals and businesses on finding their mission, I developed a process for doing so that is amazingly simple. It will work for personal or for professional life. It will work for an individual or for a corporation with thousands of employees. I would like to share this formula with you, along with some of the exercises that led me to it. As I tested this formula on myself and others, I found to my delight that people of various ages and professions emerged with a mission statement in a matter of hours, rather than months or years. People who began the process with frustrated frowns emerged from the workshop with knowing smiles. One man actually danced and swung me around with joy. Clarity is power, and thanks to this process he had suddenly gotten clear.

One association that used this technique had a reputation of being "the keepers of the flame" within a larger profession. When I reviewed their documents, their mission statement (which was five pages long and full of medical terminology incomprehensible to the average layperson) had only one consistent verb in it—"preserve." Yet when I interviewed the leadership of the organization, I found that they were not, in fact, mere museum keepers, but dynamic educators who wanted to build a whole new future based upon the tenets that had led to the profession's being founded in the first place. We simplified their mission statement to a single sentence, and added two more verbs— **promote** and **educate**. They suddenly realized that they were not merely preservers of a profession, but promoters and educators of it, as well. This simple addition of two verbs to their mission statement led them to declare that one of their goals is to become known as the premier **educators** of the profession. Upon publication of their new mission statement, the leadership suddenly found itself being invited to speak on key issues in the educational arena, whereas before they had been asked mostly to lecture on "the past." A corporation's mission statement is the single most important positioning tool it has.

In my own life I found that once I developed a mission statement that was broad enough to cover my interests and activities both on and off "the job," my life began to make a dramatic shift. Decision making came more easily, because now I had something against which to measure my activities. I learned firsthand the terror and majesty and power of having an exciting mission statement—one that says "This is what I am about." I began to shed my fears about losing or not having a job, since I knew I would always have my mission, and any job I got would have to be an expression of that.

Having a personal mission statement can help you make decisions in both your work and your home. Knowing your personal mission statement is the best career insurance you can have, because once you are clear about what you were put here to do, then "jobs" become only a means toward your mission, not an end in themselves. Having and knowing your personal mission statement can also help you navigate the mercurial world of relationships, where seemingly so few of us can exert much control. Having a personal mission statement has been shown, in fact, to be the one thing that can keep someone alive in settings as brutal and life-threatening as concentration camps.

A personal mission statement acts as both a harness and a sword—harnessing you to what is true about your life, and cutting away all that is false.

Whether we are the migrant worker turning in our last basket of freshly picked fruit, or the CEO who knows that he is only as good as his most recent quarterly report, each of us must constantly face two questions: Where now, and what next?

This book is written to address those questions: to help you define your personal mission statement, and also to give you tools that will help you accomplish it.

This book is not only about finding your mission, but fulfilling it. I believe that every theory must be proven in fact, and I have compiled case studies of people who found and fulfilled their missions, offering us incredible insight into the pitfalls and potholes they encountered along the way. At the end of the book I also share my personal experience with the frightening and phenomenal events that transpired in my own life once I sat down and wrote out my own personal mission statement.

Although I offer a formula, this is not a book about formulas. It is rather a book about process, recognizing that most people's missions will unfold as a bloom rather than take off like a bang. A mission is *evolutionary* as well as *revolutionary*, and much patience, pausing and persistence is called for along the way.

Nevertheless, people with clearly defined missions have always led those who haven't any. You are either living your mission, or you are living someone else's.

Which shall it be?

FINDING YOUR MISSION

✣ *And you will hear a voice behind you, saying "This is the path. Walk ye in it."* —ISAIAH 30:21 KING JAMES BIBLE ✣

Three Elements of a Good Mission Statement

There are three simple elements to a good mission statement.

1. A mission statement should be no more than a single sentence long.

2. It should be easily understood by a twelve year old.

3. It should be able to be recited *by memory* at gunpoint.

The truth is that all great leaders in history have had missions that were no more than a single sentence long. Abraham Lincoln's mission was to preserve the Union. FDR's mission was to end the Depression. Nelson Mandela's mission was to end apartheid. Mother Teresa's mission is to show mercy and compassion to the dying. Joan of Arc's mission was to free France. Nehemiah's mission was to rebuild the walls of Jerusalem.

A good mission statement is so easily communicated and understood that a twelve-year-old could understand and repeat it. I was recently staying at the Fairmont Hotel in San Francisco, while apparently a national casket and coffin supply company was holding its annual convention there. Outside the hotel a small group of demonstrators began chanting "Boycott mahogany! Save the rain forest!" They recited this over and over again as they marched in a circle carrying a mahogany casket. Now, I never knew there were mahogany caskets. However, as a result of my brief exposure to this group, I will be sure not to order one.

Despite what one might think about the group's methods, the chant was a most effective form of communication. They stated an action to take and a positive outcome of that action in six words. If only our major corporations, educational and religious institutions, and all people of power could communicate their mission as succinctly.

A good mission statement can be recited by memory —even if someone was holding a gun to your head. The truth is that time *is* holding a gun to our heads—pulling back the trigger and reminding us that our days on earth are numbered. We must understand the urgency and importance of our mission if we are to fulfill it.

The greater the mission, the more simply it can be stated. Yet so many companies and associations litter their mission statements with industry buzz words or such technologically complex representations that the average worker couldn't recite them if they were paid to—which, in fact, they are. At a recent leadership seminar I asked the 120 managers in attendance who could recite the mission statement of their corporation by memory. This corporation spent a small fortune in developing its mission statement, as evidenced by the elaborate, four-color, twelve-page brochure, which I had received in advance of the seminar. Of the 120 leaders there, only one could recite the mission. It was not the CEO.

Students at a medical college in California once assisted me in underscoring the importance of having a clear understanding of a mission by videotaping professors and administrators on this particular campus and asking them, live, on camera, what the mission statement of the college was. Not one person could answer the question in a single sentence. The president of the college actually asked for a few minutes so that he could run back to his office and look it up. The student reporter instead gave him thirty seconds to define it. When he could not, the reporter asked him, "Mr. President, how long have you been working here?" "Twelve years," the president replied. "You're fired," joked the reporter. The administration later actually confiscated the tape, afraid that it would become public knowledge that they did not know, and thus could not state—in a single sentence—what they were supposed to be doing.

Forgetting your mission leads, inevitably, to getting tangled up in details—details that can take you completely off your path.

A non-profit medical association whose founding purpose was to serve patients and medical students had gotten so far off its mission track that by the time the newly elected president called me in for consulting it had a travel agency, multiple real estate investments, an administrator who drove a Rolls-Royce, and a director whose full-time job it was to raise funds to pay for the prestigious high-rise office building the association had just purchased downtown—all while its patients were being underserved and its medical students were working double shifts and eating macaroni to survive.

A friend of mine was recently asked to take over the leadership of a local government-funded educational program for children. When she met with the teachers and asked to see the curriculum they had been using, they sheepishly replied that they didn't have one. "Then what have you been doing for the last two years?" she asked incredulously. *"Looking for the curriculum,"* one of them seriously replied.

I believe that all too many of us are looking for the curriculum, when in fact we should be well on our way to fulfilling and enhancing it.

Eleven False Assumptions about Missions

Before addressing the issue of writing a mission statement in detail, it is important to identify the false assumptions that can be stumbling blocks in the process.

False Assumption Number One
"My job is my mission."

Your job may be and ideally should be part of your mission, but a mission is always larger than a job. Jobs can change—and probably will. According to statistics, the average person can now expect to have four different careers in his or her lifetime. To confine the entire sum of your personality and gifts within the boundaries of your current job is to put yourself in the precarious position of losing your sense of identity when your job changes. This mindset has no doubt contributed to the phenomenon of men who die at or around the age of retirement—as was true of my father. Subconsciously they identified their mission as their job, and when their job ended, they felt they had no more reason to exist.

Down the street from me is a man who lives in a brick house. He has a brick sidewalk, a brick driveway, and brick lining for his flower beds. He is currently in the process of bricking in his side yard. Almost daily you can find him making, hauling, or laying bricks. I expect him any day now to begin bricking over his roof.

This man is an example to me of someone who needs an expanded sense of possibility. He thinks his only mission in life is bricks, when perhaps his overall passion is really landscaping.

The job you have is only the brick in your hand—it is not or should not be your only choice for landscaping. When writing your mission statement, look beyond your immediate "brick" and consider all the possibilities that lie before you.

False Assumption Number Two
"My role is my mission."

This is an especially common assumption for women. While men tend to define themselves in terms of what they do professionally, many women define themselves in terms of their relationships, or roles. While it is true that being a mother or wife can be a completely engaging task, having a role as a mission puts you in a very precarious position, because, through death or divorce, those roles can change. Many women in my mother's generation were afflicted by a depression called "the empty nest syndrome." After their children left home, these women lost their sense of identity, having believed that being a mother was their only mission in life.

My mother herself went into a deep depression after losing her mother and her elderly in-laws over a six-month period. Her role as their caretaker had been so consuming that when she no longer had them to care for, she experienced not only grief, but an identity crisis. It was only through much soul searching and counseling that she was able to redefine herself. Oddly enough, after she began volunteering with a local AIDS program, she came out of her depression, despite being surrounded regularly by death and dying. She realized that her mission was "Service," and under such a banner she could and would have multiple roles.

Your mission is always bigger than your current role.

False Assumption Number Three
"My 'To-Do' List is my Mission"

As Stephen Covey has so wonderfully pointed out

in his book *Putting First Things First*, most people's "to-do" lists fall under the realm of urgent but not genuinely important duties. Catherine Calhoun, an outstanding organizational development consultant, was commiserating with me one day about clients of hers who had gone so far as to gather information for developing their mission statements, but then decided on their own that they would go on a retreat in order to complete the task. "I know what they're going to come back with," she moaned. "Giant to-do lists based on the same priorities and urgencies they've been dealing with for the last five years. This is not their mission—to write more to-dos." Fortunately, after spending twelve hours with Catherine, they realized the error of their ways, and brought her in to do some creative, big-picture thinking.

When you are writing your mission statement, leave your "to-do" list at home.

False Assumption Number Four
"I am not currently living my mission."

I was astounded to learn that Thomas Merton, the monk whose life and writings have inspired hundreds of thousands of people, often wrote in his diary that he feared he was in the wrong monastery. A psychologist who has worked with hundreds of leaders shared the observation that many leaders do not feel powerful when, in fact, they are exercising their power at its greatest potential. The poet Sara Teasdale wrote, "I must have passed the crest long ago . . . But I did not notice it, because the thistles tore at my gown . . ."

It is highly probable that you are already living your mission at some level. The goal is to increase that awareness, so that you can live your mission to its fullest extent, rather than halfway. God told Moses that the ground on which he was currently standing was "holy ground." Your mission can begin right where you are. It need not require relocation or massive changes, but rather an increased awareness of the importance of your daily tasks and choices.

False Assumption Number Five

"I am not important enough to have a mission."

Physicists and scientists agree that even an apparently insignificant event as a butterfly flapping its wings in Africa can affect the atmosphere in Alaska. In the famous movie *It's a Wonderful Life* a suicidal businessman is shown how his existence has affected the lives of many people in his hometown by letting him see what their lives would have been like *without* him. I was profoundly affected by visiting the Simon Wiesenthal Museum in Los Angeles and viewing a timeline of historic events in the struggle for human rights. Next to such events as The Magna Carta and

The Bill of Rights is a simple inscription: *Uncle Tom's Cabin* is written by Harriet Beecher Stowe. And immediately following that inscription are the words "The Civil War Begins." A simple woman with a pen in her hand and a message in her heart changed a nation's history. Every word we speak, every action we take, has an effect on the totality of humanity. No one can escape that privilege—or that responsibility.

False Assumption Number Six

"My mission has to be a grand one or help a lot of people."

My great-grandfather was a blacksmith, and that may be why I learned early the saying "For want of a nail, the shoe was lost. For want of a shoe, the horse was lost. For want of a horse, the battle was lost." The blacksmith who kept the shoes intact in Paul Revere's horse's feet indirectly helped keep a nation from perishing. Leaders who met at the recent State of the World Forum determined that the most important jobs in the world are parenting, teaching, and healing. Yet, they lamented that these jobs are altogether too underpaid and undervalued based on the current gross national product formula for growth. If you are parenting or teaching or healing others, consider your mission among the most important in the world. Raise or teach or heal one creature, and your life can be considered a success.

"A mission must be full of suffering."

One of the most common false assumptions about a mission is that it must be hard or involve incredible suffering. Everyone has his or her bad or discouraging days, but if you feel that you can't breathe or move comfortably under your current yoke—or if you feel that you are pulling the oxcart alone—chances are you need to reevaluate your mission. When Jesus told his followers "Wear my yoke—for it fits perfectly . . . and . . . My yoke is easy and my burden is light," (MATTHEW 11:29-30) he was indicating that a divinely ordained mission is a perfect fit.

David Whyte writes convincingly of this truth in his book *The Heart Aroused.* He says that "my wants and desires were central to my destiny . . ." When he got a job he had applied for he realized, "Everything I needed for this outrageous step into a new life, including my innocent and childlike emulation of Jacques Cousteau, had been done out of a kind of sheer joy. It was exactly what I loved most that qualified me for my next step . . . I determined at that moment never to lose faith in those personal passions and desires that had led me to this oddly miraculous place of fulfillment."

Another false assumption is the belief or fear that God's will is to have you do something you don't like or aren't good at, so that, through the suffering that results, you will become humble. This assumption is very real to me. My former husband once took a job directing a church camp, without consulting me. Part of this job required that the camp director's wife be the cook. When he came home and casually slipped that fact in, I exploded. I hate cooking, especially for people with taste buds. However, I was told by him and the rest of the elders of our church that God was sending me this mission to humble me. I believed them, for a while, and even wrote an article in the national Christian women's magazine *Aglow* reporting that I was enjoying learning how to give fun names to my creations, like "Earthquake Cake," and "Pondscum Jello." The inexpressible truth was, however, that I was becoming almost suicidally depressed. Cooking for the camp wasn't my mission—it was my husband's idea of my mission.

Beware of taking on missions that fit someone else's needs—but not *your* particular interests or gifts. Sacrificial service is certainly noble, but it should be a *willing* sacrifice, not an externally imposed one.

False Assumption Number Eight
"My mission must be the same as those of my peers."

My father used to joke, usually after I returned late from a date, "You cannot soar with the eagles when you party with turkeys." When we continue to associate with people of a certain mindset, we tend to take on their values and their dreams. "Secondhand smoke kills," admonishes the Cancer Society, yet so often we determine that it is more important to be liked than to be successful—to be with the "in" crowd rather than breathe freely on our own.

In developing a mission statement that is unique to you, you must, at least temporarily, dissociate yourself from the influence of those around you, lest you become a mere follower. A "ditto head" is a character that has big ears but no eyes. Make sure you have—and preserve—your own set of eyes.

False Assumption Number Nine
"Geography is destiny."

I heard this saying several years ago, and it upset me greatly. Is it true that where you are born determines who you become? Must every young black male born in Harlem end up outlined in chalk on a city street? Must every young girl born in Iraq end up with her beauty and power veiled? It takes a village to raise a child. It also takes a village to stifle one.

The point of geography's influencing destiny is never more obvious than in examining what artists paint, and thus, what they became famous for. I like to study the change in artistic style that took place in the artist Georgia O'Keeffe after she left New York City. While she was in New York her art was comprised of dark, somber tones. She painted gray buildings and black smokestacks and shadows of skyscrapers. Once she saw the wide-open skies and muted pastel colors of the West, her entire style changed— from a stark realism to her "sky is the limit" wild expressions of blues and greens and tans and yellows.

Your landscape or cityscape is affecting you in more ways than you realize. Jesus talked about the importance of guarding what your eyes take in—because what your eyes take in becomes part of you. Make sure what you are seeing on a daily basis is the right context for the destiny you want to make for yourself. Obviously, if your mission is to serve the poor you probably won't be living in Aspen, Colorado. The point is, there should be a natural and positive alignment between your mission and your geography. Don't let geography alone determine your destiny. Let it be part of your supporting backdrop.

Make sure when you are writing your mission statement you are aware of the influence of your physical surroundings, and look beyond the borders or boundaries that geography might seem to impose on you.

False Assumption Number Ten

"What I am doing is as close as I can get to my real mission."

One writer recently observed that many people enter careers that shadow or parallel their real dreams. You could get rich if someone gave you a dollar for every English professor, ad agency copywriter, newspaper reporter, editor, or literary critic whose real dream is to be a full-time novelist, playwright, or a screenwriter. I know—because I was one of them. As a child I had declared that my goal was to be able to make a living through my writing. With my ad agency I was indeed doing that. Yet one day after writing an ad for a hospital I felt so angry and frustrated that I tossed my copy across the desk. It wasn't that the ad copy wasn't good. The problem was that it was "good enough" to keep paying my bills, and thus allow me to continue to live in the shadow of my real dream. I wanted to write messages from my heart, not just polish up somebody else's.

Look carefully to see if you are taking a job that runs parallel to your true heart's desire and mission—but is not actually *it*. Go for what you want <u>directly</u>. Beware of parallel imitations that look like, but are not, the "real thing."

False Assumption Number Eleven

"Life is random. Even I was an accident."

As someone who was constantly assured by my family that I have an important destiny, it came as quite a surprise to me when my mother shared the story of how I very nearly didn't come to be. It seems her mother's mother had been given in an arranged marriage to a much older man in

Germany—a man who not only beat her but forced her to bear children almost immediately to help him with his work. By the age of twenty-six she had six children, and a miserable life. Fortunately for me, she met a young dreamer who spoke of starting a new life in America. He invited her to come with him, and one night she packed her bags, and sailed for the United States. Their "love" child, my grandmother, was then born and raised in New York, and unfortunately married a violent man who forced her to have three abortions. She lied to him about the fourth abortion, and when he returned from his travels to discover that my mother had been born, he argued so violenty with my grandmother that my mother—a two-year-old—was injured when she came between them. My grandmother left him the next day, and my mother grew up as an only child of a single mother in New York. Mom grew up and eventually headed West, seeking wide-open skies. She was on her way to California when her car broke down. While it was being fixed, she met my father. They fell in love, married, had my sister, then had me and my brother.

I asked my mother not long ago to help me plan my life. She smiled and said lovingly over her cup of tea, "Honey, how can I help you plan your life when I didn't even plan you?" I went out that night and looked at the stars for a very, very long time. This psalm came to mind.

MEDITATION

O Lord, you have examined my heart and know
everything about me. You know when I sit or stand.
When far away you know my every thought. You
chart the path ahead of me, and tell me where to stop
and rest. Every moment,
you know where I am. You know what I am going to
say before I even say it.
You both precede and follow me, and place your hand
of blessing on my head.

This is too glorious, too wonderful to believe! I can
never be lost to your spirit. I can never get away from
my God. If I go up to heaven, you are there; if I go
down to the places of the dead, you are there. If I ride
the morning winds to the farthest oceans, even there
your hand will guide me, your strength will support
me. If I try to hide in the darkness, the night becomes
light around me. For even darkness cannot hide from
God; to you the night shines as bright as day.
Darkness and light are both alike to you.

You made all the delicate, inner parts of my body,
and knit them together in my mother's womb. Thank
you for making me so wonderfully complex! It is

amazing to think about. Your workmanship is mar-
velous—and how well I know it. You were there
while I was being formed in utter seclusion! You saw
me before I was born and scheduled each day of my
life before I began to breathe. Every day was recorded
in your Book!

How precious it is, Lord, to realize that you are
thinking about me constantly! I can't even count how
many times a day your thoughts turn towards me.
And when I waken in the morning, you are still
thinking of me!

Search me, O God, and know my heart; test my
thoughts. Point out anything
you find in me that makes you sad, and lead me
along the path of everlasting life. ✖

(PSALM 139: 1–18, 23–24. THE LIVING BIBLE)

Forming a Sense of Mission

Contemplate the Big Picture

It would be foolish to undertake such a mighty task as determining one's mission in life without first contemplating the overall scheme of things. If you want to know where you fit into the picture, it would be wise to begin by looking at the picture itself. Yet contemplation involves meditation and reflection—activities that are becoming a lost art in a society that is fascinated with technology and action.

I have to admit that meditation is especially difficult for me. I long ago determined that my legs were not meant to be pretzels, and the word "Om" was something I used to get dinged for uttering at Toastmaster's meetings.

The truth is, I have never been able to fully empty my mind. But I am quite capable of losing it.

I lose it—or "loosen it"—whenever I am riding my horse named Desert Star out among the cotton fields. I "loose it" when I am standing in a hot, hot shower, letting the water sting and stimulate and "sensate" my back. I lose it when I sit with my mother and watch the clouds billow and mushroom and bloom over a Sedona sunset sky. I lose it when I see sunlight hitting a reed tipped by a red-winged black bird. When I am most aware of the beauty in God's world is when I lose my mind.

Sufi poet wrote, "The universe surrenders to a mind that is still." And in order to truly find The Path, each of us must loosen our minds, and begin from a point of wonder and openness—of being willing to *not* know. We must receive, before we can begin to give.

Thich Nhat Hanh, a monk from the Far East, recently shared with me that the most important gift anyone can give is "a mindful presence." He told me how he takes three deep breaths, and then says to the moon, "I see you, moon. I am aware of your beauty, and I sense your pain. And I am here for you." He believes that if everyone would do this with their spouses and families and friends and animals and even the rocks and trees, the world would be a more peaceful place.

So I suggest that while contemplating the overall scheme of things, and your particular part in it, you take three deep breaths, and then say "I see you, World. I see your beauty. And I sense your pain. And I am here for you."

As we open ourselves, the answer will find us. In fact, the answer is already on its way.

Isaac went out in the fields in the evening to meditate, and when he looked up, behold, the camels were already coming. GENESIS 24: 63 . KING JAMES BIBLE

Your Mission Will Fit You Perfectly

Your mission will be perfectly suited to your personality. In his poem "Two Tramps In Mud Time" Robert Frost wrote lines to this effect:

> My object in living is to unite
> my avocation and my vocation
> As my two eyes make one in sight.
> Only where love and need are one . . .
> and the work is play for mortal stakes
> is the deed ever really done for heaven
> and the future's sakes.

FROM THE POETRY OF ROBERT FROST

When I encounter teachers who are constantly complaining or meet housewives who are bitter, I quickly conclude that they are not following their *divinely* ordained mission. Perhaps they are following their *economically* ordained mission, or their *culturally* ordained mission, but they can't be following their *divinely* ordained mission, because bees hum while they work—they don't whine.

I believe it is well within the natural order of things to have everybody humming while they work. As a noted economist recently stated, "Unemployment is a characteristic unique to the human species only. All the other creatures and creations seem to know what they are supposed to be doing."

People cannot find their missions until they know themselves. Even Jesus had to go out into the wilderness to get clear about who he was and to take the full measure of his gifts. The fact that he was able to describe himself afterwards in single-word pictures is a testimony to the power of self-knowledge and self-esteem. "I am the Light," He said. "I am the Way. I am the Vine. I am the Good Shepherd. I am the Gate." He had a multitude of powerful and positive images that communicated to both himself and others who he was.

A recent article in *USA Today* noted that the advertising slogan and song words "Like a rock" became the theme that transformed Chevy trucks from being unreliable to top sellers in the nation. The workers kept the image of "a rock" in their heads as they produced the automobiles. This new, powerful "self-image," reinforced constantly through song, is credited with leading to the corporate turnaround.

What we think about ourselves is clearly and unequivocally reflected in everything we say or do—in our work, our surroundings, our family life, and our service to others. Therefore it is important to take the time to get a more clear picture of who we really think we are.

The following exercises, which are suitable for both companies and individuals, are designed to help you with that process. It is advisable to enlist a "Mission Partner" for this task—someone who you know and trust, and who has no agenda in the outcome of your life (i.e., preferably not a boss, spouse, or competitor). The purpose of the Mission Partner is to complete each of these exercises about you. Have them write down which element in their mind most describes you, and then compare and reflect on their answers.

Exercise:
Think about the four elements: Earth, Water, Wind, and Fire. Which one are you most like?

I am _____.

List at least twelve characteristics this element has.
For example, Wind is: invisible, powerful, untamed, moody, unpredictable, exciting. . . .

Now describe what that element does. List at least twelve actions or verbs that apply to it.
For example, Wind: soothes, blows, comforts, pollinates, excites, stirs. . . .

Take your name and insert it before your element.
Ex. I, _____, am wind.

On a separate sheet of paper write down all the characteristics you listed in the second and third exercises. At the end of this list write down your name again as you did at the top of the list. You have now created a powerful word picture about yourself.

Repeat this "poem" daily for thirty days, adding new words as they occur to you.

DISCUSSION:

There is a very practical application to these meditations, which I discovered when the element I chose for myself was Water. During the time I was doing my thirty-day meditation on "Water," I encountered someone who was so

Neanderthal in his thinking I was sure that I could see scrape marks on his knuckles. He made some comments to me that were so offensive, so uneducated, and so bigoted that I was literally speechless after his attack. When I went back to my room after our meeting, I was seething. My mind quickly went to work determining which of my various relationship tools I could use to render him incapable of reproducing.

Having gone through my inventory and finding any number of weapons that were suitable, I decided to stop a moment and pray. I remembered my meditation on Water. And it was then as if I heard a Voice saying to me, "Laurie, I called you to be Water—not stone against stone." That message, along with the word picture of water, did more to hasten the forgiveness process than any angry prayer I could have forced myself to say, gritting my teeth while doing so. I literally saw myself as water going over this stone, making a happy bubbling noise as I went over his head. Thanks to the word picture of me being water, I was freed.

Exercise:
Draw a word picture about yourself that is not an element. For example: I am a bridge . . . or, I am an eagle . . . or, I am a doormat. Describe the first image that springs to your mind, without editing its content.

DISCUSSION:

The pictures that come spontaneously to our minds are often gifts full of messages. One man in my seminar, a very well dressed, successful executive, turned pale and admitted that the word picture that came up for him was "I am Humpty Dumpty." That image conveyed instantly and powerfully his current state of mind and feelings of lack of support.

Another man who said, "I am an acorn" was part of an intensive group seminar I conducted that met over a period of six weeks. At the beginning of each new session the participants would stand and share their word pictures. During the course many people found that their "I am" pictures changed. Young Eric, however, kept maintaining that he was "an acorn." Someone in the group finally challenged him, and asked, "Eric, how long do you want to go around being a little nut? At what point are you willing to become the oak tree you were meant to be?" After further dialogue with the group, which included a frank discussion regarding his fears about responsibility, Eric began to acknowledge himself as "an oak tree."

Imagine for a moment how your dealings with people would differ if you considered yourself as: a.) an acorn b.) an oak tree.

How you view yourself is how others, also, will see *and* treat you.

I love the scripture that says, "We shall all be changed in the twinkling of an eye." (1 CORINTHIANS 15: 51-52) I like to read it as, "We shall all be changed with the twinkling of an *I*." The Gospel is full of hope and messages about the grace we are given to become new creations. We each definitely have a part in that process. We can change, and be changed. If you do not like the word picture that comes up for you, imagine its opposite and ask for the grace and strength and power to make the new picture reality.

MEDITATION

by Laurie Beth Jones

I am earth—
the soil that supports
and nurtures living things.
I give solid footing
to those around me.

I am wind—
the power that
sweeps away old fears
and carries new ideas
like springtime.

I am fire—
igniting the power
and passion in others.
I give warmth
on cold, wintry nights,
and clear the way
for new beginnings.

I am water—
irresistible.
No obstacle can stop me.
I go over, under,
around and through.
I change forms
to steam or ice
or rain.
I bring life
wherever I go.
I touch everyone
I meet.

Who Are You?

Personalities with a Past

None of us exists in a vacuum (and some of us, like myself, don't even have one). If it is true that we are a product of the DNA that resides within us, then it seems only logical that we are also formed by PPI—the Past Personality Influences that have combined to make us who we are.

Barbara Shur offers excellent insight into this fact in her book *I Could Do Anything—If I Could Only Figure Out What I Want*. In one of her exercises she asks the reader to write down what each of the following relatives wanted you to be: father, mother, grandfathers, grandmothers, aunts, uncles, siblings. Then she invites the reader to draw a composite picture of what that person so described would look like, if all those expectations managed to take shape *in only one person*.

When I did the exercise I learned some interesting things about myself. My composite drawing showed a woman carrying the scales of justice, a sword of courage, a typewriter, a tennis racket, a torch, various trophies, a thesaurus, a turkey dinner for the homeless, and a briefcase, preferably full of money. She was standing at a podium reading from the Bible, had one foot in high heels, and the other in tennis shoes. She was wearing blue jeans under her fully fashion-coordinated two-piece suit, and had a spiffy red sports car waiting for her when she got out the door, which, given her load, was not likely to happen without a great deal of help.

After drawing the ideal composite self based on his family's expectations, one of the men in our seminars shouted out "I have become exactly what my mother wanted!" Despite this revelation, he admitted that he was very happy in his life and his chosen profession. Sometimes our family expectations can be good ones. The important task is to sort out which ones fit the real you, and which ones don't.

Carl Jung said, "Nothing affects the environment of a child so much as the unlived life of a parent." Consciously or subconsciously we each pick up the frustrations our parents felt. Some researchers suggest that we were even influenced by our mother's emotions when we were in her womb. Therefore, in the process of discerning your path, it is important to sit back and reflect on both your Past Personality Influences and your parents' "unlived lives."

My father wanted to be a social worker, but after the War, he realized there would not be enough money to support a family, so he became a salesman instead. My mother was studying art at Pratt Institute in New York and had dreams of becoming an artist until the Depression hit. She became a bookkeeper instead, and for thirty-five years she worked with numbers instead of paintbrushes. Circumstances had come crashing down around my parents that seemed to shout NO! to their dreams. I, like many of you, resolved subconsciously to live out my parents' unfulfilled dreams. I often wonder if their "unlived lives" became the tool that shaped me even more than the actual careers they chose.

A close friend of mine who grew up on a ranch in Mexico was told even as a little girl that "Someday this ranch will be yours." Her father had worked hard to earn the money to buy the ranch until finally, it was theirs. She remembers riding with him for miles on horseback to mend a fence or fix a windmill. One day he fired a ranch hand who had been caught stealing cattle. The next day, the ranch hand gunned him down, shooting him in the back as he got into his truck. The tragic death of her father at the age of forty-two affected thirteen-year-old Maggie in more ways than she could measure. She immediately went to work to help her mother, who was left with five children, against a government that wanted that land. Despite her mother's best efforts, and the exhaustion of the family savings in order to pay all the *mordidas*, or bribes, which were the only way of doing business in Mexico at the time, the family lost the ranch. Three hundred thousand acres. Stolen by the government.

The family found solace in their faith, and Maggie went on to college—mastering in social work and theology. She became actively involved in church work in the city, determined to fight injustice at the spiritual level.

Last year, when she was 49 years old, a close family friend gave her a horse. Unable to refuse this generous gift of a beautiful stallion, she was suddenly "forced" to go riding again. When she did, there entered into her soul a sense of well-being she never seemed to find in the paperwork demands of her job.

Being on that horse seemed to bring it all back to her. She is now making plans to open a riding stable with several partners—and has purchased a home near open fields that stretch as far as the eye can see. She has also initiated a campaign to try to get the family's ranch back again.

Clearly, she did not bury her father's dream when she buried him.

Exercise:

1. What were your parents' unlived lives? Do you know what their dreams were? Write them down.

2. Have their unlived lives affected or influenced you? If so, how?

3. Picture yourself standing in a room. One by one the following people come up to you, look into your eyes, and hand you a gift. What is it?
   Your Father (or father figure)
   Your Mother (or mother figure)
   Your Grandfather(s)
   Your Grandmother(s)
   Your Aunt(s)
   Your Uncle(s)
   Your Stepfather
   Your Stepmother
   Your Brother(s)
   Your Sister(s)
   Your Priest, Rabbi, Pastor, or spiritual leader

4. The same people also hand you a cup filled with something that caused them sorrow, pain, or concern. What is in the cup of pain or sorrow that each person hands you?

5. Which of the cups of sorrow are you unwilling to drink?

6. Which cup are you willing to drink, or have you been drinking from?

7. Which of the gifts that were given to you have you chosen to use?

8. Which of the gifts have you chosen not to use?

The Power of Positive Prophecy

It is said that the grandmother of Jackie Joyner Kersee named the child Jackie, "Because someday she is going to be first lady of something!" Because she grew up in an atmosphere of positive prophecies and expectation, this child, who later overcame a birth defect, went on to become the first lady of track and field.

One of the most important things we can do for others—and for ourselves—is to create and maintain an atmosphere charged with positive prophecies. While not all of us were fortunate enough to have parents or grandparents or families who gave us positive prophecies about ourselves, I believe that God always offers a compensating balance of grace to us. I believe that somewhere, sometime, someone offered you a positive prophecy about yourself. Perhaps it was a comment that shocked or surprised you.

Perhaps it was an observation that you automatically dismissed out of foot-shuffling humility. But if you think back, I would be willing to bet that you can remember some encouragement that had been given to you—a compliment that, if believed, could be used as a key to unlock your destiny.

One man shared in my workshop that although he grew up in a rough neighborhood, the elderly man who ran the dry cleaner always told him he was a very smart boy, and would someday grow up to run a big business. Billy, who came from a family of abusive alcoholics, somehow clung to this life raft of hope about himself, and climbed onto it. He became the chief financial officer of a multi-million-dollar health care entity despite his family's negative example, and perhaps because of one man's positive prophecy —*which he chose to believe.*

Another woman shared that she grew up in poverty in New York, but would always find her way to one of the office buildings that had a fancy elevator. "The woman who ran the elevator would let me ride up and down with her for hours. She would tell me how smart I was, and that someday I was going to be a very important office woman myself." Despite a background of poverty this woman is now an attorney in a very prestigious law firm, perhaps because of one woman's positive prophecy.

Occasionally, someone will give us a negative prediction, which, viewed rightly, can be transformed into a hurdle that makes us stronger. "My high school teacher told me I could never play football because I was too skinny. I got so mad about it that I started weight training, and two years later, made varsity. I'll never forget seeing him in the stands the day I caught my first pass and made a touchdown," shared Ken, a now muscular man who laughed with satisfaction at the story. "My teacher's negative prediction became just the spur I needed to get me into shape."

In each of the above cases, success came directly as a result of the person's *chosen reaction* to the prediction or prophecy. Too many of us choose to ignore the many signs about our destiny that God is sending us through other people.

Exercise:

1. Write down a positive prophecy someone gave you about yourself. It could be recent or from years ago.

2. Who was the messenger?

3. Has their prophecy come to pass?

4. Could it still?

5. Whose voice can God use to reach you with messages about your mission and destiny?

6. Can you recall a negative prediction someone gave you that actually became fuel for you?

Finding Your USP

People who work in advertising are taught to look for, and communicate, the USP, or Unique Selling Point, of a product. There is or should be something that makes this product distinctive, and it is their job to find it. My favorite story about this principle concerns an agency rep who was assigned to come up with a campaign to boost sales for a popular laundry soap. Given a week's deadline, he found himself under a great deal of pressure. The product had been a strong seller for nearly twenty years. What could he say that was new about it? He poured the soap out onto his desk and began to look at it as if for the first time. He noticed it was full of little blue crystals. When he asked the client what the blue crystals were, he was told that they supplied the super-whitening, brightening agents that made the soap so effective. The campaign the rep developed was "Try Tide—With the New Blue Crystals." Sales shot up significantly, all because someone threw a spotlight on a quality that had always been there. He found Tide's USP.

In order to get on your true path, you must first identify your own USP. What is it that makes you unique? We've been told since sixth-grade biology class that there is no one like us and never will be. Our fingerprints, our voice prints, our DNA are so distinctive that we could be singled out from a crowd of millions by means of just those few physical characteristics.

Our spiritual and mental and emotional talents and gifts make us equally special. There has never been a package like you ever before in history, nor will there ever be again. Let's look at the package, and see what's in there.

A good place to begin the search for your USP is childhood. William Wordsworth said, "Our birth is but a sleep and a forgetting." We forget at birth, perhaps, who we were in heaven—and the gifts we had there. Sometimes the memory of who we "were" in heaven before we "are" on earth lingers through childhood.

Willy, my artist friend, remembers drawing pictures even when she was still in diapers. Her mother confided to me that they could not keep crayons or paper away from her, or she would wail to the heavens. "The only way we could keep her quiet in church was to let her draw," recalled her mom with a smile. Willy was drawing from the time her fingers could fit around a crayon. It came naturally to her.

Judy Missett, the founder of JAZZERCISE, states that she knew she wanted to be a dancer at the age of *two*. Julie Castiglia, my literary agent, says when she was little she couldn't get her hands on enough books. She would surround herself with books on her bed, on the floor, and in the hall. "I loved the smell of them, the feel of them in my hand. No wonder I do what I do!" she laughed.

Terry Moore, a man from Kentucky, wrote and told me that when he was a little boy he used to have his brother bring him magazines, which he would scatter on the family pool table and then pretend to conduct "board" meetings. He now runs a successful construction company.

My little brother used to play for hours in the tub, looking for his planes and submarines "until the water got so dirty he couldn't find them." Now he is a flight scheduler for a major airline, coordinating a department that keeps track of every aircraft they own. His computer screen looks like a three-dimensional chessboard. "With radar, I can locate every plane we have," he said. "Even when the sky gets too dirty?" I joked. "Yes, even then," he grinned.

"Unless you become like a little child, you cannot enter the kingdom of heaven," Jesus said. Perhaps it is worthwhile to go back to our childhoods, and open up the trunk where we kept all our toys. Perhaps we were aware of our paths, even then.

Exercise:

1. What did you do for fun when you were a child?

2. What were your favorite toys?

3. Your favorite games?

4. Do you remember anything that came particularly easy to you as a child?

5. What did you tell people you were going to do or be when you grew up?

6. Are you being or doing anything that resembles that dream now? If so, what? If not, why not?

Looking at Your Gifts—Today.

One of the reasons many of us don't recognize our gifts *as* gifts is because they seem so natural to us. The concept that we must earn a living by the sweat of our brow, and/or put our nose to the grindstone, contributes to our overlooking the fact that our destiny can actually involve doing something that we love to do, or that comes easily to us. When people say "Oh, you are so good at this or that," we often automatically dismiss what may be a profound perception on their part.

The famous Santa Fe artist and woodcarver Ben Ortega was a farmer who, as a hobby, used to carve wooden saints. One day the community held a fund-raising craft fair, and he donated one of his hobby carvings of St. Francis. So many people ordered the piece that he had to quit farming and take up carving full time to meet the demand. He found his mission in life by giving what he loved away—doing something that came easily to him.

Wally Amos of "Famous Amos Cookies" fame found the same route—baking cookies for friends as thank you's, and ending up with so many orders that he had to start a company to meet the demand. Neither of these men sat down and thought—*I will be a woodcarver*, or *I will be a cookie maker*. They simply shared their gifts, and the path opened up before them.

We have all been given many gifts. But it is our responsibility to use and multiply them. It is also our responsibility to expect fair wages for the gifts we use in our work.

Two parables Jesus told speak strongly to this fact. A landowner gave out various talents to three men. One man buried his, fearing reprisals should he lose what he had. The other two took what they had and multiplied it. When the owner appeared, he punished the one who buried his talent (and thus engaged in a self-fulfilling prophecy). The ones who actively sought to improve and multiply what they had been given received a rich reward. "For the person who uses well what he is given shall be given more, and he shall have abundance. But from the man who is unfaithful, even what little talent he has shall be taken from him." (MATTHEW 25: 29. THE JERUSALEM BIBLE) We must use our talents, or lose them.

Jesus told another parable that illustrates our responsibility regarding our work life.

The owner of an estate went out early one morning to hire workers for his harvest field. He agreed to pay them $20 a day and sent them out to work. A couple of hours later he was passing a hiring hall and saw some men standing around waiting for jobs, so he sent them also into his fields, telling him he would pay them at the end of the day. At noon and again around three o'clock in the afternoon he did the same thing. When all the men gathered to be paid, they each received $20, even those who had been hired in the latter part of the day. The workers hired earlier protested, saying "Those fellows worked only one hour, and yet you've paid them just as much as those of us who worked all day in the scorching heat." "Friend," he answered one of them, "I did you no wrong! Didn't you agree to work for $20?" (MATTHEW 20: 1–13. THE LIVING BIBLE)

The parable speaks of God's generosity, but it also implies that *we will get what we settle for*. We must value ourselves, and our talents, at their proper worth.

Exercise:

1. People say "Oh, you are so good at_____."

2. Write down a list of no less than twenty talents you have been given. Pretend that you

will be given a $1,000 bill for every talent you list.

3. Which of those have you buried?

4. Which talents have you multiplied?

5. Whom are you blaming for your talents being buried?

6. Who does God say is responsible for the development of your gifts?

7. Draw a shield with four separate, equal parts in it. In each part, draw a symbol of your four most cherished talents. (This is the shield you will take with you as you carry out your mission.) For example, my shield has a pen, a heart, a pair of lips, and wings, denoting my gifts of writing, feeling, speaking, and the freedom to do all of the above.

Your Passion Is Your Power

The exercises on the previous pages have helped you focus on your unique gifts and background. These exercises are designed to help you focus on your *passion*. If your mission holds no personal passion, it is not your path. Enthusiasm comes from the root words "en" and "theos"—which means "in God." What are you enthusiastic or "in God" about?

Exercise:

1. What most excites you in or about the world?

2. What most angers you in or about the world?

3. If you could teach three things to others about what excites you in the world, what

three things would you teach? For example, if you picked "beauty" as what excites you, you might want to teach these three things: That beauty is all around us. That we must preserve and protect it. That it takes time and training to recognize and appreciate it.

4. If you could convey to others three things about what angers you in the world, what would you convey?

5. How can you use what most *excites* you to affect or change what most *angers* you? List at least ten ways.

The What of it all

Every mission requires action, and action words are verbs.

Exercise:

Below is a list of verbs. Pick out the three verbs from each page which most excite you. Then from that list select the ultimate three. These are the action words which will shape your future activities. (Note how the words form the shape of a candlestick on each page. It is the verbs we choose to act on that shed light on who we are.)

accomplish
acquire
adopt
advance
affect
affirm
alleviate
amplify
appreciate
ascend
associate
believe
bestow
brighten
build
call
cause
choose
claim
collect
combine
command
communicate
compel
compete
complete

compliment

compose

conceive

confirm

connect

consider

construct

contact

continue

counsel

create

decide

defend

delight

deliver

demonstrate

devise

direct

discover

discuss

distribute

draft

dream

drive

educate

elect

embrace

encourage

endow

engage

engineer

enhance

enlighten

enlist

enliven

entertain

enthuse

evaluate

excite

explore

express

extend

facilitate

finance

forgive

foster

franchise

further

gather

generate

give

grant

heal
hold
host
identify
illuminate
implement
improve
improvise
inspire
integrate
involve
keep
know
labor
launch
lead
light
live
love
make
manifest
master
mature
measure
mediate
model

mold

motivate

move

negotiate

nurture

open

organize

participate

pass

perform

persuade

play

possess

practice

praise

prepare

present

produce

progress

promise

promote

provide

pursue

realize

receive

reclaim

reduce

refine

reflect

reform

regard

relate

relax

release

rely

remember

renew

resonate

respect

restore

return

revise

sacrifice

safeguard

satisfy

save

sell

serve

share

speak

stand

summon

support

surrender

sustain

take

tap

team

touch

trade

translate

travel

understand

use

utilize

validate

value

venture

verbalize

volunteer

work

worship

write

yield

Write down your three most meaningful, purposeful and exciting verbs here.

_____ ,

_____ , and

_____ .

These three verbs comprise puzzle piece # 1.

What do you stand for? What principle, cause, value, or purpose would you be willing to defend to the death or devote your life to? For example, some people's key phrase or value might be "joy" or "service" or "justice" or "family" or "creativity" or "freedom" or "equality" or "faith" or "excellence." What is your *core*? Write the word or phrase down here.

_____ ,

This becomes puzzle piece # 2.

Whom Are You Here to Help?

Every mission implies that someone will be helped. A nation will be freed, a bird will be returned to its nest again, a child will have a new image of what parental love can be. Whom is it that you were sent here to help? The more specific you can be, the more focused and powerful will be your energy.

Jesus said, "I came to help the lost sheep of Israel" and was reluctant to turn his attention to the Gentiles, knowing that someone would follow in his footsteps to undertake that specific task—namely, Peter. Because he was clear on his "for whom" he stayed within a 30-mile radius of his home, teaching, healing and preaching primarily to "the lost sheep of Israel." His specific "for whom" enabled him to keep his focus.

A friend of mine who had been working strictly with environmental organizations wanted to broaden her base of concern. She realized that the core values of the organizations she wanted to serve were those of non-profit institutions—groups who were devoted to causes that did not have financial gain as their first prerogative. The "for whom" that she selected for her mission statement was, therefore, "non-profit agencies."

A man named Gedalia who came to one of our seminars billed himself as "The Ambassador of Romance." He even offered to sing in exchange for his price of admission. Suspecting that seminar participants would not be interested in hearing romantic Julio Iglesias–type songs as they worked on their mission statements, Dee, my administrator, made other arrangements with him for payment. As we went through the list of whom he really wanted to help, what evolved was that his passion was for children—getting them excited about music. The fact that he was making his living singing in nightclubs had caused him to think of, and bill, himself as "The Ambassador of Romance." Singing in nightclubs was his current job, but it was not his mission. When it became apparent that what he really wanted to do was work with children in the public school systems, his mission statement became clear. His "for whom," then, was not "romantic couples" but "children in the public schools."

Get clear on who you really want to serve, be around, inspire, learn from, and impact in a positive way.

Below is a list of groups and/or causes. Pick the three that most attract you.

Environment
Family Issues
Education
Media
Health Care
Elderly
Children
The Poor
The Homeless
Immigration
Energy
Agriculture
The Justice System
Parks & Recreation
Veterans
Substance Abusers
Nutrition
Law
Politics
Government

Youth
Roads & Bridges
Business
Non-profit Agencies
Churches
Synagogues
Spirituality
The Ill & Disabled
Public Safety
Human Development
Infants
Child Protection
Child Care
Justice
Home Health Care
Water Rights
Tourism
Defense
Space Exploration
Animal Rights
Animal Care
Animal Protection
Labor Relations
Literacy
Border Issues
Civil Rights Issues

Sexuality Issues
Fashion
Art
Books
Music
Movies
Design
Sports
Food
Computer Technology
Administration
Management
Construction
Labor Relations
Travel
Finance
Real Estate
Printing & Publishing
Religion
Community Development
Reproductive Issues
Research
Biotech
Women's Issues
Gardening
Broadcasting

News
Journalism
The Performing Arts

Pick the *one* group, entity or cause you most would like to
help or impact in a positive way. Write down that cause,
entity, or group's name here.
This becomes puzzle piece # 3.

Putting it all together.
This is the formula for your mission statement.
Puzzle Piece #1 + Puzzle Piece #2 *to, for, or with*
Puzzle Piece #3.

My mission is to:
_____, _____, and _____,
(your three verbs)

_____,
(your core value or values)

to, for, or with

_____,
(the group/cause which most moves/excites you)
(Puzzle Piece #3)

DISCUSSION:

Does this surprise you? Is it similar to what you have been doing? If it's different, how is it different? How do you feel when you look at it? Say it out loud. Does it fit you? Is it exciting enough to move others to help you? Do others agree that this suits you? Does it have "heart"? Now get a thesaurus and a synonym finder and write down as many possible words that relate to the key words in your mission statement. This will give you an expanded sense of the possibilities before you. For example, the key words in my mission statement are:

Recognize, inspire, and promote

What does it mean to recognize? What does it mean to inspire? What does it mean to promote? How many ways are there to recognize, inspire, or promote divine excellence? I developed a long list of all the possible words relating to those key words. This list later helped me develop my action plan.

One person asked me "What if I come up with the wrong mission statement?" When I asked him what his current mission statement was, he didn't have one. I told him, "Well, whatever you come up will be 100 percent more accurate than the one you have now." I strongly believe that once we set our feet on a path, we will be corrected

and guided as long as our hearts stay focused on integrity—
both ours and God's.

Checking your mission statement

A good mission statement will be inspiring, exciting, clear,
and engaging. It will be specific to you and your particular
enthusiasms, gifts, and talents. If the mission statement you
came up with does not meet these criteria, rework it until
it does.

Remember that a mission statement should be
large enough to encompass a lifetime of activities. As I
stated in the book's introduction, Jesus said that his mission was "to give life, and give it more abundantly." All
his activities flowed from that mission: Turning water
into wine. Healing the sick. Raising the dead. Teaching
others. Throwing or attending parties. Challenging the
"enslaving" religious system of that time. I challenge any
reader to find one action of Jesus that did not flow from
or relate back to his stated mission of and passion for
"abundant life."

*Our mission statements should be as powerful and all
encompassing.* Make sure all your activities can flow from
and relate back to your mission.

Your Mission Statement Should Cover Both Work and Personal Life

A woman in one of my seminars wrote that her mission was

"to raise a happy family."

That might have covered her personal life, but it left her work life unaddressed. It also left her responsible for something she could not control, which was the happiness of others. A broader, more encompassing mission statement we wrote together read:

> My mission is to create, nurture, and maintain an environment of growth, challenge, and unlimited potential for all those around me.

This accounted for both her work and personal life, and left her free to continue her mission once her family was raised. It also more clearly defined her area of responsibility as being that of *creating an environment*—something she *could* control, as opposed to *raising a "happy" family*—something she would probably not be able to control on a daily basis.

I once asked a man who was known to have ulcers when he felt he would be happy. "Not until everyone in my family is happy," he stated with conviction. This man had *thirteen* brothers and sisters. He had virtually doomed himself to a life of dis-ease by claiming as his mission something he could not ever control. Remember, one of the definitions of mission is "a clearly defined territory of responsibility."

A CEO that I worked with could initially only state that his mission was "to create a profit for my shareholders." This left his personal life unaddressed. The statement we rewrote together read:

"My mission is to foster innovation, enhance cooperation, and create prosperity for all whom I serve." This mission statement allowed him the flexibility of doing these activities both at work and at home, as well as broadening the base of his activities.

A young woman who works at a cancer care center wrote her mission statement as being:

To inhale every sunrise, and look under every rock
for the joy life has to offer.

It came as no surprise to me to learn that the day after she wrote down her mission statement, she won the "6:30 A.M. Sunrise Run" sponsored by the local hospital. Her mission statement covered both her personal and her professional life.

A man at the same seminar drew hoots of laughter when he shared that his mission statement was simply "to finance love." (Talk about a mission statement with potential for limitless activities—he had one!)

When someone in the group challenged him to explain how that statement covered both his work and personal life, he smiled.

"My mission is 'to finance love' because I work in the accounts receivable department of a non-profit hospital, and 'to finance love' also covers my personal life because I am getting married in January."

Matching Your Mission to Your Employer's
If your mission statement does not match or closely relate to the mission statement of the place where you are employed, prepare yourself for ulcers, sleepless nights, and countless hours of complaining (either by your boss, your co-workers, or your stomach).

In my ideal world employees would know the mission statement of the company they served, and all corporate executives would know the mission statements of the people who serve them. Each would complement the other.

A man who is a labor relations expert developed the following mission statement in a recent workshop I gave.

> To uphold, discover, and support
> trust, honesty, and integrity in all relationships.

He shared that he had left a lucrative career at a university hospital because, in his words, their mission was only two words "Prestige and money." He went to work for a smaller, less well-known hospital whose mission is "to serve and heal others in the ministry of Christ." Terry said that he has never been happier at work than he has been at this Catholic Charities hospital even though the work he is doing there is basically the same, and is as challenging as what he was doing at the university hospital. He is happier because his mission statement found a match with his employer's.

Judy, another employee of the hospital, came up with the idea of having a "missions book" placed in the chapel, where anyone who wanted to could share and also read about the mission statements of those who serve in the hospital. She also visualized each person's mission statement being written on a brick, and each of those bricks being used to build the foundation for the new building. She captured with her imagination what actually is or should be happening with every company. *The personal mission statements of the employees are the only sure foundation of any larger entity.* Do you know the mission statements of your employees—or employer? If not, how solid can the work be that you are doing?

Unsuccessful or Inadequate Mission Statements

Unsuccessful or inadequate mission statements will have these characteristics.

1. THEY ARE UNINSPIRING.

   Examples of these are mission statements or phrases such as:

To survive.

To exist.

To get by.

To retire by the age of fifty-five.

2. THEY ARE FOR THE BENEFIT OF ONE PERSON OR
PARTY ONLY.
Examples:

To conquer Europe.

To beat Nebraska.

To own a Mercedes.

To put the competition out of business.

3. THEY ARE UNINTELLIGIBLE BY "OUTSIDERS."
Examples:

One mission statement I read recently was for a
religious art foundation. It was eighteen para-
graphs long, contained a brief summary of the
history of the Renaissance period, and yet never
did say what it—the foundation—was here to
do.

4. THEY ARE FULL OF TRITE OR ORDINARY PHRASES.
"We are here to serve our customers." This has
become so overused that it is boring. . . . Serve
them how? Serve them when and where? Why
are you serving them at all?

Creating the Vision Statement

While a mission statement is centered around the process of what you need to be doing, a vision statement is the end result of what you will have done. It is a picture of how the landscape will look after you've been through it. It is your "ideal."

Your vision statement is the force that will sustain you when your mission statement seems too heavy to endure, enforce, or engage. All significant changes and inventions began with a vision first.

It was the vision of Christopher Columbus returning to Spain with ships full of spices, converts, and gold that led Queen Isabella to grant him the money for the journey. She surely would not have granted him the funds if he had approached her with "I need three ships, lots of men, lots of money, lots of time, and maybe I'll get back to you." This was actually the *reality* of the situation, yet Columbus sold her on the vision first. The details became almost insignificant.

The founding fathers who met in Philadelphia envisioned "a more perfect union based on life, liberty, and the pursuit of happiness." They did not write down "We are going to lose our land, our lives, our fortunes, and everything we've worked for while trudging through mud, enduring freezing cold, and dying from lead bullets." This was the reality of what happened to many of them. Yet it was the vision of a free land, shimmering in the not too distant future, which kept them loading their muskets and pushing their mules and eating hard tack and sipping soup.

The proverb "Where there is no vision, the people perish" emphasizes the need we have to be able to envision the future. Our very existence depends on it.

Yet most of us are still caught up in the past. Few of us can see beyond the present. Each of us *must* see into the future, and thus help create it, if we are to successfully accomplish our mission.

Physicists are now aware of subatomic particles that hover in and around everything that exists. One interesting characteristic of these particles is that they seem to take on the properties or expectations of the scientists studying them. This has led to the speculation that these particles may be the creative building blocks of the universe. All mass is surrounded by hovering possibilities waiting only to be spoken to in order to become. God said "Light be, and Light was."

If these particles surround us all, then each of us is currently and constantly creating the future by what we say and think *whether or not we are aware of doing so.*

It is imperative then that we get clear about what we *are* creating and compare it to what we *intend* to create. The only way to do that is to:

a. look at what we've consciously or subconsciously created up till now and then

b. write down a detailed description of what we really want.

The key elements of a compelling vision statement are these:

—— IT IS WRITTEN DOWN.
Don't trust your memory to help you remember it. Most of us can't even remember where we left our car keys, much less what the land of milk and honey looked like when we were in a high state of creativity. Keep it where you can refer to it daily.

—— IT IS WRITTEN IN PRESENT TENSE, AS IF IT HAS ALREADY BEEN ACCOMPLISHED.
The mind only thinks in "now." It does not

know any other tense. The mind duplicates exactly what we say or think. If you say "I will try to do this tomorrow" it will replicate the state of "*trying* to do something," which is, in actuality, not having done it, and putting it on the shelf of "tomorrow"—which never comes.

——It covers a variety of activities and time frames.

Be sure you've covered weekend activities as well as weekday tasks. Anything you forget or neglect to color in will remain "uncolored in."

——It is filled with descriptive details that anchor it to reality.

The mind thinks in pictures. Colors, fragrances, and sounds help its recall. It anchors events or images with multiple details. Give your mind the details it needs to make this vision seem very real. Some people do "mind maps" which have pictures resembling the house or car or feeling they want to create.

Jesus emphasized the importance of being specific in our requests. The man who got a stone instead of a fish from his father probably said, "Oh, I don't care. Just give me anything."

I often visualize heaven as being like a catalog fulfillment center, full of angels reading requests. "This one reads 'I want to be happy in the future,' says Gabriel. "What exactly does that mean?" asks Michael. "I don't know. What should I do with it?" asks Gabriel. "Put it in the 'hold' file, with all the rest. Someday maybe these humans will learn to be specific," sighs Michael, as he marks yet another request "incomplete."

In the previous chapter I spoke about Gedalia, the Ambassador of Romance who really wants to be the Pied Piper of Music for Children, who refined his mission and his slogan during one of my workshops. His mission statement read:

My Mission is to enliven, encourage, and
reinspire the love of music for children in
public schools.

His Vision statement looked something like this:

I am singing three nights a week and spending the

rest of my time working in the public schools. Once a month I organize and attend school assemblies which feature my work and that of other musicians. As a result of the work that I have done, children in North County have attended three free concerts this year, have increased enrollment in band participation by 30 percent, and have personally met and talked with singers and musicians who are enthusiastic about their work. There is a resurgence of the sales of folk music in local music stores, and two corporate sponsors now provide scholarships for music classes for the underprivileged. I have received sponsorship for my work through private funding, and am being approached about taking the model of what I do statewide.

Gedalia's mission and vision statement were so clear and compelling that he attracted three volunteers to help him by the end of the seminar. Once you get clear about what you want, you will begin to attract help from multiple sources.

Leadership trainer and author Dave Cowan recently told me a fascinating story about gravitational pull. Apparently most of the fuel that is used by spaceships traveling to the moon is consumed in just getting them beyond earth's gravity. After they have done so, NASA scientists count on lunar gravity to pull the spaceship toward the moon. Similarly, it is "escape velocity" that requires most of the energy, moving us away from our former way of life. A compelling vision must be so clear and so powerful that its very magnetism and gravitational forces will literally *pull* you toward it.

Authors Michael Hammer and James Champy state in their book *Reengineering the Corporation* that the only companies that seem to successfully negotiate the arduous process of change are those that have created and communicated a very clear vision of the future, aided by statistics and projections of what would happen if the company *didn't* change.

The Bible itself begins with a compelling vision of the Garden of Eden. It ends with the hope and possibility of our having heaven once again on earth, providing we make the necessary changes. (It also includes a fiery description of what could happen if we *don't* change.)

Exercise:

Project where you will be in
- three years,
- five years,
- ten years,
- twenty years
—if you merely maintain the status quo.

If you don't like what you see, what is your preferred future? What is your ideal?

Realize Your Point of Power

Author Robert Fritz teaches that the very moment you realize you are unhappy or frustrated with a situation is your "point of power," for now you have a clear picture of how you *don't* want things to be. Imagine the exact opposite of the frustrating situation, and there you have the makings of your vision.

When I began working in the advertising industry, it quickly became apparent to me that some clients tended to take advantage of our relationship, asking for free proposals full of creative ideas that they would then take and execute on their own, or using the ad agency as a scapegoat to blame when their poorly strategized marketing plans or products failed. I actually had one client lambaste me over the phone because the sales of his sofas dropped, despite the fact that we were not advertising sofas—at his request. Every job and industry has its frustrations, but I determined early on not to be in or tolerate any relationships with clients which I felt to be abusive.

After my unhappy experience in advertising, I wrote the following as my vision statement: "I have clients who delight in and cherish me, and who properly value my creative talents and efforts. We are mutually engaged in serving others. My clients come exclusively through referrals, allowing me to be free to devote my energies to creating. They are doing work or offering products that I respect. They pay me well and on time. I have long-term relationships with the people I serve, and they are as interested in my well-being as they are their own." I then "anchored" it by adding—"It is Monday morning, 10 A.M. I am wearing comfortable clothes, having returned last week from a major consulting job. I sit down in my home office and catch up on work from the week before. For lunch I walk down to the park for Chinese food. When the phone rings it is another referral. I set up an appointment for the following week. When I open the mail it is filled with checks."

When I shared this vision with an associate at a local advertising federation meeting, she scoffed, "Dream on, Jones. You might as well not be in business." I disagreed however, and found another associate who supported me in my vision. He even mused, as we were walking along the beach, "See all those seagulls swarming around that fishing boat? They are like your future clients. They're going to be chasing you!" I appreciated and believed his positive prophecy, and would recall it on those days when not even sparrows seemed to be limping around my car.

Once I wrote out that vision statement for my work, things definitely started changing. I began to attract clients with similar values and tastes as my own. When I combined the vision statement with my mission statement (which was "To recognize, promote, and inspire divine excellence") I had a yardstick to use in measuring my activities and determining daily responses to situations that developed.

Get Into Conscious Creating

Jesus told us to be specific in our requests, and urged us to "fear not, for it your Father's *good pleasure* to give you the kingdom." One philosopher states that the purpose of our life on earth is to learn that our thoughts have power. William James wrote that the greatest discovery of this century is that by changing our thoughts, we can change our lives. We are constantly thinking, and every thought is filled with creative power. We are constantly creating, but most of it is done unconsciously. The purpose of a vision statement is to get us into *conscious creating*.

In the delightful movie *Princess Cariboo*, a young woman in England imagines herself to be a princess from a distant island country. She goes so far as to create her own language, her own flag, her own costumes, and her own heritage. Her mannerisms, her stance, her gracious and refined hand movements speak truly of a noble birth. She is so convinced that she is this princess that the entire town begins to believe her—with hilarious and revealing results. At one point she has all of London's royalty learning her exotic native dance, following her around the room in a conga line, mimicking her rolling and swaying movements.

Bankers begin to explore using her as an ambassador

to help raise money to invest in the island. A royal duke proposes to her—believing he can expand his territories, and upgrade his personal image, as well. The women begin to dress like her—enchanted that they have been visited by royalty.

The entire fantasy comes tumbling down when a suspicious reporter uncovers the fact that the country the princess claims to come from does not exist, and rather than her being of noble, foreign birth, she is a common, wayward girl from London with no family at all.

When she is interviewed by the reporter, the princess explains, "But you see, when I thought about the princess, I really *became* her." Ultimately, the entire community is transformed, recognizing that for some reason, they needed her to be a princess to make them feel better about themselves. The reporter falls in love with her, and they sail off to America—the land where everybody seems to have, and live, their dreams.

Create a Vision for Your Relationships

A compelling vision statement can also help guide us to effecting change in the most difficult and challenging arena of relationships. While we cannot control or dictate the behavior of others, a vision statement about how we wish to conduct ourselves, and the "tone of being" that we desire to maintain, will definitely become a sifting and filtering device, a necessary protective boundary, and a magnet for others.

Bebe had been involved in an unhappy relationship. She finally took the time to write out in her journal exactly what her vision of the ideal marriage would be. For her it involved having a husband who was supportive of her career, who loved to cook and do housework, someone who had his own career, and enjoyed staying at home, fixing or building things. Being a firm believer in the power of the written word, she also wrote her vision statement out in her Day Timer and referred to it regularly:

> *It is Friday afternoon, 5:30 P.M. My husband picks me up from the airport with champagne on ice. We drive to our newly constructed home, and have dinner, which he has lovingly prepared. After dinner we walk down the two steps to our sunken living room, and sit in front of the fire, have wine, and talk about our day.*

After reading her vision statement, I ignorantly suggested that maybe she lower her sights a little bit, as: a) she traveled all the time, and thus had little opportunity to meet "a homebody," and b) I'd never even *heard* of a man as romantic and domestic as that. Undaunted, she kept to this statement and took it out to read it over every few weeks or so. Three years passed. Then one Christmas eve she called me and said, "I've met the man in my vision."

Ed is not only a gourmet cook but owns his own construction firm and had traveled so much in his former career that he hates to leave town. He is also a former boxer and current cycling champion. Happily single for the past twelve years, he is the father of her daughter's best friend, and actually lived around the block from Bebe. They did not meet until my friend wrote down her vision statement, and shared it with someone else—in this case, her daughter. Bebe and Ed have now been married for ten years and have built a new house with "two steps down into the sunken living room." He not only picks her up at the airport with champagne on ice, but brings her tea on a breakfast tray every morning. Bebe claims that her marriage is even better than she imagined. The point is, she *did* imagine it, the beginnings of it, and wrote it down.

Two women were having a discussion, one of whom was happily married and the other wasn't. The unhappily married one shared, "I can't even imagine such a happy life," to which her friend gently but firmly replied, "Perhaps that is why you don't have one."

Jill, a friend and colleague of mine, was married to an apathetic, beer-guzzling, chronically unemployed husband. After several months of exchanging pleasantries and surface conversation, she finally admitted to me that she was unhappy, but had uncertain feelings about leaving Al, as he was the father of her two very young children. One Sunday I invited her to accompany me to look at a pony I was contemplating buying for my stable.

As we arrived a family of four also drove up. The husband and wife were dressed for church, and their little five-year-old girl and seven-year-old boy were wearing jeans, boots, and cowboy hats. As his wife helped their son get on a pony, the man confided to us that his wife used to raise horses, and since they had been restationed at the nearby military base they had not had a chance to even be around horses. "After we get a pony for the kids," he said, "she doesn't know it but I'm going to buy her a horse, too. This way she and the kids can ride together while I'm gone. I couldn't wait to get up this morning to come out here! I was more excited than the kids!"

They did, indeed, purchase the pony, and as he was writing out the check the man smiled to us and said, "You should see my wife on a horse. I think she was born on one!"

As we were driving off Jill said wistfully, "I want a family life like that. My husband sits around on Sunday watching TV all day. We never do anything together like go to church, the park, the movies."

Seeing an opportunity for a new vision statement for my friend, I whipped out a pen and paper and said, "Let's write it down."

So over lunch she constructed a new vision for her family life, one that read:

> I have a husband who can't wait to get up to do things with me and the kids. He loves to plan surprises for me, and is constantly thinking of ways to make our life happier and more fulfilled. We are doing things together as a family. He is proud of me and my talents, and verbally praises me in front of other people.

When she shared this vision with her husband, he mocked her and stomped out of the room, slamming the door as he left. Within two weeks she moved out—recognizing that she needed space in order to make her vision come true. When I asked her if she was afraid, or was getting lonely without Albert, she said, "When I do I just get out the picture of him sitting on the couch drinking beer, and I reread my vision statement, and I know I'm doing the right thing."

Jill cannot change her husband. But she can change her standards of acceptance. And she alone, with God, is responsible for setting the tone in her life.

Not to have your own vision is to live somebody else's. When we were discussing how Jill got into her mess, she wondered, "Why would I allow myself to pay all the bills, do all the housework, even carry in the fifty-lb. bag of dog food, while he simply sat on the couch and drank beer?" She paused for a moment, and then burst into a laughter of recognition. "I was living *his* vision!" she exclaimed, shaking her head. "I didn't have a vision of my own." Ideally, both people in a relationship will have the same vision—and will work toward it with an equal amount of commitment and dedication.

Ironically enough, Jill's move prompted major changes in Al. He is now attending AA meetings, going to church, and spending every free moment taking the boys fishing or to the park. He also got a new job. Last week he even asked her what her dreams were, and agreed to write down his, as well. She may or may not go back to him—but her vision is close to coming true—*ninety days later!*

A Vision Statement Is a Recruiting Tool

Jesus, one of the greatest recruiters of all time, gave very clear vision statements about what would happen to people who worked with him. "Drink my words, you will never be thirsty again." "Abide in me, and you will be like a living vine—always bearing fruit." "If anyone comes to me, he will be born again—and will be a new creation." He also spared no words about the challenges that would confront them.

Vision statements like these became his recruiting

tools. People who wanted the same pictures for their own lives came to serve him.

The president of one of the largest manufacturing companies in the world is adamant about recruiting people who have proven a commitment to his company's mission, which is "To Serve God in All We Do." He therefore recruits heavily through pastors around the world—people who know young men and women who have already given their lives to God. Michael's reasoning is this: "I can always teach people the business. But we cannot afford to spend our time trying to teach people values."

Having a clearly articulated vision and mission statement will be a terrific magnet and filtering device. It is possible to persuade other people to see the wisdom in *your* vision, as well.

In the book *How to Argue and Win Every Time*, author and trial lawyer Gerry Spence writes that in gaining a victory for one of his clients, he told the jury, "After your deliberations, I want all of us to walk out of this courtroom as free people. I want to walk out as a free person. I want you to walk out as a free person. And I want my client to walk out as a free person, knowing justice has been done." He relates that after the jury did indeed free his client, one of the jurors came up to him and said, "Thank you for telling us so directly what you wanted. That was what we all wanted, too, and your words made it all come together for us." Asking them to find his client not guilty would not have been nearly as powerful as creating in their minds a picture of his client walking out of the courtroom as a free man. He gave them a vision they couldn't refuse. Spence exalts "the power of the honest who tell us who they are and what they want!"

"Imagination is everything," wrote Albert Einstein. When you are writing out your vision statement, think about a world where, "With God, anything is possible." Color outside the lines. Look at people who are having, being, doing, creating what you want to create as role models.

Exercise:

Questions for Individuals

1. Who is living the life you most envy?

2. Describe what you think it is like.

3. Who is doing the kind of work you most wish you could be doing?

4. Describe what their work life must be like.

5. If you only had six healthy months left to live, what would they look like?

6. What do you want more of:

—in your relationships
—in your work

7. What do you want less of:
   —in your relationships
   —in your work

8. Describe in detail your ideal work setting.

9. Describe in detail your ideal work day.

10. Describe in detail your ideal co-workers.

11. If money were no object, what would you be doing with your life?

12. What would you do if you were ten times bolder?
    • In your primary love relationship?
    • In your work setting?
    • In your community?
    • In your family?
    • In your place of worship?

13. Imagine that it is Monday morning, 9 A.M., three years from now.
    • Where are you?
    • What are you doing?
    • Who are you seeing?
    • What are you wearing?

14. It is now noon, same day.
    - Who are you going to see?
    - Where are you going for lunch?

15. It is now Saturday, 6 P.M.
    - Where are you?
    - What are you doing?
    - Who are you seeing?
    - What are you wearing?

16. You are now a very old person, walking with a school child who asks you, "What are you most proud of about your life?"

17. You are about to die. What did you accomplish before you left?

18. As a result of your having lived, three things have changed or shifted in the world. What are they?

19. Now write out your vision statement, incorporating your responses from all of the questions above.

Exercise:

Questions for Companies, Groups, or Associations (using "group" as the common entity)

1. What do you, as a group, want more of?

2. What do you, as a group, want less of?

3. Describe the kinds of relationships you wish to have with:
   - your customers
   - your suppliers
   - your shareholders or investors
   - your competitors
   - your community
   - your peers
   - your employees

4. The newspaper honors you as "Company of the Year." In the article they highlight your:

5. Your product or service is meeting what critical need in the:
   - community
   - marketplace
   - region
   - world

6. Your company has changed the history of: (check any that apply to your vision)
   - the community
   - the marketplace
   - the region

- the world
- other _____

7. It has done this by:

8. Your company or group has been called "A Light on a Hill." This is because:

9. Now write out your vision statement, including activities, states of being, and desired accomplishments.

Sustaining
Creative Tension

Once you have formulated your vision, a new kind of work begins: the important task of keeping that vision as the dominant thought in your mind. This takes conscious mental discipline, for too many of us have a "lazy eye" when it comes to maintaining a vision before us.

In the movie *Apollo 13*, the astronauts were able to guide their crippled spaceship home using little more than battery power, as long as they kept the vision of earth in their window. Having lost their sophisticated navigational equipment, their hope of returning was reduced to one harsh but simple truth: If they lost sight of earth, they would be lost forever. The commander's job became to keep the vision of their destination always within sight.

I was fascinated recently to look at the television screens that have a "picture within a picture"—small image of the program from one channel is superimposed over the corner of the image of the channel being watched. The person viewing the screen can therefore take in information from two channels at once. Although it is obvious that this technology was created almost exclusively for football fans, I find it a useful model for how we must begin to "see" in order to facilitate making our visions real. We must look at the picture from WCI (What Currently Is) on one channel, while still seeing the picture of WCB (What Could Be) on the other channel—the channel of the future.

True visionaries must be able to simultaneously input and integrate the two channels at once. Robert Fritz calls this process—holding up *what is* next to *what could be*—"Sustaining Structural Tension." He says that the mind has one desire, and that is to see only one image. It therefore goes into overdrive trying to integrate the two, and it will put most of its energy toward the picture that is most often viewed. Therefore, people who focus only on "what is" will create more of "what is." People who focus mostly on "what could be" will begin to create "what could be."

The tension in this process is, for many people, unbearable. Unwilling to handle the stress of seeing two disparate images, they will "take down" or "turn off" the vision of the future, and thus slide back into the status quo.

This principle is reflected in the saying, "The rich get richer, and the poor get poorer." Why would "The one who has, receive more, while the one who has little, see the little he has taken away," unless they were both getting what they were focusing on? "As you believe, so shall you receive."

A personal example regarding my initial experiments with this principle involved making money. Workshops have always been turning points for me, and after attending Robert Fritz's workshop on "Technologies for Creating" I then attended a course on money management. In this course we were challenged to look at our attitudes about money. As a Christian who had been indoctrinated that the love of money was the root of all evil, yet as a person whose father's dominant concern was that I be extremely financially successful, I was torn internally about how to handle money when I got it.

In the course we were taught that money is a neutral object. Like fire, it can be used to heal, light, warm, or burn. It is merely a reflection of the people using it. As one of the exercises we were asked to write down what we would like to make or earn in the upcoming year. At the time I was a salaried employee earning $36,000 annually. I felt comfortable with this, as I had learned that this figure was the *combined* income my parents had earned while I was growing up. When the instructor came by my chair and noticed that I hadn't written anything down, he asked me why my sheet was blank. I said, "I don't know what to write down." He said, "Laurie, there is no 'wrong answer' here. Why not just make a figure up?" Looking down at my Day Timer, I noticed (not for the first time) that it was soon to be the year 1986. "Okay," I replied, almost flippantly. "I want to earn $86,000 in 1986!" The class applauded me, and I dutifully wrote the figure down on the card that had been provided: "My income is $86,000." We were instructed to keep the card in front of our names for the remaining five weeks of the course, so that everyone walking by would comment, "I see that you earned $86,000 this year. Good work." "Oh, yes," I would reply in the spirit of the game. "It was much easier than I thought."

After the class ended we were to take the card home and place it in an area where we would look at it first thing in the morning and as the last thing at night. By putting that card on my bathroom mirror, I had now entered what I call "the creative tension zone." Suddenly all sorts of things began to change, the first being that I became extremely dissatisfied with my current job. I was at the time in a quasi-partnership with a man who wanted me to launch an ad agency for him in San Diego. As the year unfolded I began to realize that although I was getting the clients, he was scooping off the profits. When he finally violated a profit-sharing agreement we had made, I resigned. So now, instead of earning $36,000 a year, I suddenly had no salary at all. This all happened within one month of my leaving the "money course." Great work.

However, most of our clients opted to go with me in my new solo venture, so I had a base. I also networked like crazy. I attended 7 A.M. networking meetings and didn't get home until 10 P.M., having gone to back-to-back receptions for one group or another. I had pockets full of business cards. And things began to hum. I had almost forgotten about my $86,000 goal. In fact, once I resigned, I had actually taken it down off my mirror, believing it would be too unrealistic to think I could nearly triple my income my first year in business.

Yet six months into my venture, I totaled up all my sales, and the figure, amazingly enough, came to $42,000. "I am almost halfway there!" I realized with a shout. I whipped out the vision card and put it up again, this time taping it down on the top *and* bottom. By the time the year ended I had earned more than $86,000. That is how I became such a firm believer in the power of writing things down. I was the same person, loved by the same God, yet I had finally gotten very specific in my goals and requests.

Earning the money had involved lots of hard work, but it *had* been easier than I had imagined. I found that the creative tension zone is not such a bad place to be, if you're staying busy and working toward your dream.

Fritz and other writers and philosophers observe

that those people who succeed are the ones who can not only handle but actually thrive in the creative tension zone. Like Michelangelo who took a rough piece of marble and chipped away everything that did not look like the vision of David he held in his mind, we must realize that the majority of our time as artists, writers, managers, leaders, parents, teachers, and healers will be spent carving and sculpting in the studio, getting dust in our eyes, rather than out on the podium, receiving applause.

Once you have a mission statement and a vision, you, too, will have entered the "creative tension zone." The point to remember is that life is always filled with tension and stress. When you are working on your mission and vision, however, you are experiencing *creative* tension, rather than *random and meaningless stress* brought about by choosing to live according to someone else's vision.

Exercise:

1. Pretend that you are Michelangelo, and you find yourself standing before a block of hand-selected, but rough-cut, marble. As you begin to chip away the stone, think about what your David or vision of inspired creativity will look like.
   - What is it that must be chipped away?

- What is the tool, or tools, you will be using?
- How often are you working on your statue?
- Who comes to visit you while you are working?
- What do they say as they see you at work?
- What would you like them to say?
- What could keep you from completing the statue?
- What else might keep you from completing it?
- How long are you willing to work on the statue?
- How are you feeling while you are working on it?
- How do you stay focused on its creation?
- What kind of support do you need to finish it?

2. After writing your vision statement, pretend that your mind is like those television screens that have a small picture framed within a larger picture. Which frame is the larger one—

a. your future, or your past?

b. the problem, or the solution?

c. what is, or what could be?

3. Study the drawing below. Place yourself as a large dot somewhere on the drawing.

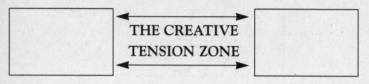

THE CREATIVE
TENSION ZONE

What is now: Your ideal vision:

FULFILLING YOUR MISSION

❧ Commit your work to the Lord—and your plans will be established. PROVERBS 16:3. KING JAMES BIBLE ❧

The Eight Action Steps
to Success

Once you have your mission written down, and you have the vision clearly in mind, these eight steps will take you through the creative tension zone. In this section I will introduce each step, and in the following sections I will share case studies of well-known people who used these eight steps in accomplishing their missions.

Get the facts.

Know more about the situation you're facing than a reporter who is writing a major article would. Do your homework. I once met a gentleman who had enjoyed an amazing rise to power in the dangerous and precarious world of politics. He had been appointed to key positions by both parties. When I asked him the secret to his success, he said, "I made it my business to know more about the subject at hand than anyone else in the room. And," he added with a smile, "you'd be amazed at how simple it was to do that." Too many people assume that they know, rather than that they *don't* know. Wisdom comes from realizing how much you don't know, and taking the time to get the facts.

I was once hired by a cardiologist to help him recruit a general practitioner for his practice. Seeing that the trend was toward increasing funding for general practice and decreasing funding for specialists, he had decided that what he needed on his staff was a good GP. Before I got on the phone to my sources, I met with the office staff and did some investigative research. Where were this doctor's referrals coming from? Who were his major customers? Surprisingly enough, 87 percent of his practice came from referrals from local general practitioners. Armed with this fact, I sat down with him and asked him if he was prepared to immediately replace 87 percent of his business the day he hired his own GP. He turned pale and said, "No, of course not." Yet, had he not gotten the facts from someone, he could have made a major mistake—one that could have cost him hundreds of thousands of dollars, just because he was acting on an idea he had after reading an article. The man is a genius cardiologist. Yet even he didn't know the facts about his own practice. Never assume that you know. Check. Ask. Research.

Questions.

1. How much do you know about your "mission field"?

2. What is your source of knowledge?

3. When was the last time you updated your knowledge base?

Get a goal.
Boil your mission statement down to the single most important goal or task. Write down clearly what your goal is—preferably in five to six words. For example, in the case studies that follow, Queen Esther's mission was to save the Jews. Her single most importan *goal* was to get the king to reverse his decision. Nehemiah's mission was to *strengthen* the Jews. His single most important *goal* became to rebuild the wall. Moses' mission was to free the Jews. His first *goal* was to convince Pharaoh to let the people go.

In the example just mentioned above, the cardiologist changed his goal from "Hire a General Practitioner" to a new, more practical and relevant one, which was "Increase Referrals." Your mission statement and your vision statement should be able to be boiled down to tangible, achievable, and clearly communicated goals. (Remember: "Boycott mahogany. Save the rain forest.")

1. What is your main goal?

2. Is it written down?

3. Have you communicated it to others? Could they recite it verbatim?

Examine, educate, and enlist your resources.

Your resources consist of such things as your time, your talents, your gifts, your hobbies, your training, your material wealth, your environment, and most especially the people that you know who also have all of the above.

You would be wise to "inventory" all your resources, including the names in your Rolodex. It is so easy—too easy—to overlook the resources you have right at hand. Yet your mission's success will depend on how strategically you engage those resources. Know who and what they are. Educate them about the mission. Then enlist them in the mission, making sure you clearly communicate what is in it for *them*.

I once worked with a woman who had decided to start her own industrial supply company. As we talked about her business plan, she asked how much it would cost to develop a marketing and advertising campaign for her new venture. Having learned from experience that I can serve clients better after we've reviewed the Eight Action Steps together, I automatically began the process with her. When we came to this step, #3, I asked her to write a list of everyone she knew in business. At the top of the list was her father, who owned a huge construction company. When I asked her if she had told him about her idea to open her own company, she said no. When I asked her why not, she said that she just hadn't gotten around to it. I suggested that before we went any further she should show her plans to her father. She did, and he immediately put her in touch with someone who gave her so much business that she didn't need to advertise.

Questions:

1. Make a list of your resources. Include such items as:

Time

Talents

Training

Health

Finances

Friends

Hobbies

2. Make a list of all the people you know who

might be able or willing to help you with your mission. Are you aware of *their* total resource base?

3. Ask these people to help you. Communicate why it would be good for *them* to help you accomplish this mission.

Turn old business into new business.

One of the sayings I wrote in my journal recently reads, "I have learned that if love was ever there, love is *always* there." Anyone who has ever helped you, or cared about you, or bought something from you is a potential resource that can be rekindled and engaged in helping you with your mission. We are so often out chasing the new idea or the new customer that we forget about the old ones we had who still have a lot of breath—and buying power—in them. Before you go out hunting a new team, go through your Rolodex and review the list of people who, at some level, even if just through knowing you, were on your team before. You will save a tremendous amount of energy, and perhaps accomplish more with these people than you did the first time you worked together.

Questions:

1. Which contacts from your past might be willing to help you again?

2. What dreams or talents did you once have
   that could be "reawakened?"

3. What could you do to rekindle a fire that has
   almost gone out—
   a. with your customers?
   b. with your family?
   c. with your significant other?

Give them something tangible to remember you by.
Napoleon said that the greatest discovery he ever made was
that men would be willing to risk their lives for the privilege of wearing small medals on their chests. It seems that
during every major battle in history a flag was flown during
the fighting—something the men could look up to and be
inspired by. In the upcoming case history of Joseph, Joseph
was thrown in prison and in a magnanimous gesture interpreted a fellow prisoner's dream. When his prophecy came
true and the person was freed, Joseph called out,
"Remember me to Pharaoh." Yet it was two years before the
man had an occasion to remember Joseph. When Pharaoh
had a dream that he didn't understand, that's when the
man recalled Joseph. My premise is that if Joseph had had
a brochure, he wouldn't have had to wait three years for the
man's memory to go into recall.

I recently received, via Federal Express, a small, credit-
card–size tape recording device. A man who had read

Jesus, CEO was so anxious to get in touch with me that he sent me a recorded message on the machine. Of all the messages and correspondence I received that day, guess which got answered immediately? This man had given me something tangible to remember him by. It was one of the most creative forms of communication I'd received.

Questions:

1. What tangible things do you give people to help them remember you by?

2. How many of those are unimaginative and ordinary?

3. How could you be more creative in getting your message across—and making it memorable?

Break ranks. Be bold.
Every leader mentioned in this book had to step out from the crowd and quit marching in place. Yet so many of us are like the children calling out "Mother, may I?" before taking the steps that will win the game. Be bold and brazen about what you have to accomplish. My journalism teacher taught us that it was often better to beg forgiveness afterward rather than wait for permission beforehand when it came to getting a story.

My father used to say that the shores of time are littered with the bones of those who hesitated, and having hesitated, lost.

Be bold. Step out. Do it now. Picture in your mind that the suspension bridge you are standing on is disappearing beneath you. Make that leap you need to make as *if your life depended on it.*

Questions:

1. Where, and why, are you currently marching in place?

2. Who is going to give you permission to take the step you need to take?

3. What would you do if you were ten times bolder? Go out, and do it.

Get visible.

In order to succeed you and your mission must be seen and heard. The laws of attraction in nature are based on visibility. A bullfrog hops high and croaks loudly to let the lady frog know where his pad is located. Birds sing to attract the feathered friends of their dreams. Flowers blossom and bloom in an explosion of colors to both release and receive the pollen that will ensure their survival.

I was once attending a weeklong conference at a very

nice hotel—one that had peacocks lounging around the grounds. One day as I was walking through the lobby I saw two teenaged boys staring, mouths open, at the window. There, not a foot away, was a male peacock with his feathers in full display. His tail was arched forward, and his entire fan, which was nearly five feet high, was quivering with iridescent intensity. The boys and I both said "WOW!" in unison. One of the boys turned to me and said, "Had you ever noticed that bird before?" I answered, "No, I hadn't." The other one shook his head and said quietly, "But he's been here all week." Pretend that until now you've been just an ordinary bird, dragging a long tail. What will it take to hit the switch that puts your feathers in full array?

Questions:

1. What are you doing to become visible?

2. Who offers a positive example of visibility in your community or workplace?

3. Are you a mousy mudhen, or a proud peacock, when it comes to sharing your mission?

Saturate everything you do with prayer.
Prayer has been called the most powerful source of energy known to man. It offers a direct line to God and has been

described by various psychics and visionaries as uniterrupted streams of light pouring from the heart and mind of the petitioner. Jesus spoke of it often, and used it unceasingly in his own endeavors. Prayer opens us up to receiving the divine help which surrounds and envelops us on a constant basis.

Since the human will was created as something inviolate, even to God, and since Jesus spoke of politely standing at the door and knocking—not barging in like some celestial Rambo—it stands to reason that God also waits to be asked, invited, and received. Ever mindful of the human need and desire for independence, God aften stands by, like an all-knowing parent, waiting for the child to ask for help. It is no coincidence that the ordinary citizens of earth who became legendary in scripture bathed their missions and actions in prayer. They sought the help, and guidance, of the Divine. Jesus said "My father's house is a house of . . . prayer." (MATTHEW 21:13)

Review some of the guarantees given regarding the results of prayer:

MATTHEW 21:22 "You will receive whatever you ask in prayer."

JAMES 5:16 "The earnest prayer of the righteous person has great power and wonderful results."

JOB 22:27 "Pray to the Lord, and he will hear you. Fulfill your promises to him. Whatever you wish will happen. And the light of heaven will shine upon the road ahead of you."

When Jesus said, "I am the vine, and you are the branches," he surely must have seen prayer as the force that keeps us connected to him, and he to us. Saturate everything you do with prayer.

Case Studies

Nehemiah: Man with a Mission

Nehemiah is one of my favorite examples of a person with a mission, because his story offers multiple illustrations about what happens when a person becomes passionate about a cause, and the obstacles he has to overcome in order to accomplish it.

In December 446 B.C., a man named Nehemiah was serving as a cupbearer to King Artaxerxes of Persia. Nehemiah was at the palace when one of his kinsmen, Hanani, arrived with some men from Judah. "I asked them," Nehemiah said, "about the Jews—the remnant rescued from captivity—and about Jerusalem. 'Those who escaped from captivity,' they replied, 'who are back there in the province, are in great trouble and humiliation; the walls of Jerusalem are in ruins and its gates burned down.' On hearing this I sank down and wept. For several days I mourned, fasting and praying before the God of heaven."

Nehemiah poured his heart out to God, saying that he acknowledged that the reason the Jews were scattered is because "we refused to obey your laws." Yet he asked, "O Lord, hear my prayer. Heed the prayers of those of us who delight to honor you. Please help me now as I go in to ask a great favor from the king."

King Artaxerxes noticed a change in Nehemiah's demeanor. He no longer seemed enthusiastic about his job. "I took up the wine and offered it to the king. Now I had never been downcast before." So the king asked, "Why is your face so sad? You are not sick, surely? This must be a sadness of the heart."

Despite Nehemiah's trembling fear, a fear that almost overcame him, he told his story to the king. "May the king live forever. How could my face be other than sad when the city where the tombs of my ancestors are lies in ruins, and its gates have been burned down?"

"What," the king asked, "is your request?" "I called on the God of heaven," Nehemiah relates, "and made this reply to the king, 'If it pleases the king, and you are satisfied with your servant, give me leave to go to Judah, the city of my ancestors' tombs, and rebuild it.' The king and the queen asked, 'How long will your journey take, and when will you return?" So I named a date that was acceptable to the king, and he gave me leave to go." Nehemiah pressed him further, asking for letters that would allow safe passage, and also for timber for the city walls and the house he was to occupy. This the king granted as well as an escort of army officers and cavalry.

Nehemiah had previously been happy with his job. However, the fact that he was willing to look beyond the palace walls and inquire about the condition of his brethren led him to his great mission. His heart was heavily burdened by the condition of Jerusalem, and he fasted and prayed for guidance on what to do about it. I find it interesting and enlightening that he did not just walk up to the king the following Monday morning and say, "Take this job and shove it!" Yet many people do exactly that when they leave their current jobs in order to serve a new, more passionate mission. Because Nehemiah first sought the Lord's help and then went with respect to his employer, his employer granted him a generous leave of absence. Obviously, this king was a wise and kind man, and not everyone has such a caring and considerate boss. Yet Nehemiah had helped nurture and cultivate his relationship with his boss to the point of mutual concern and intimacy. Nehemiah never treated his former boss with disrespect, nor did he kick sand on his old job when he left for a new one.

So, Nehemiah had his calling, his boss's blessing, an official escort, and even a big purchase order for the Royal Treasury. What could stop him now? The next sentence describes what happens to all of us when we set out on our journey, flush with confidence. "When Sanballat the Horonite and Tobiah the Ammonite slave came to know of this, they were much displeased that anyone should come to promote the welfare of Israel." The drama has been set. There are always enemy forces who will work against you when you attempt to change the status quo.

Nehemiah arrived in Jerusalem and stayed there three days, "not telling anyone what work God had inspired me to do." Under the cover of darkness he quietly and on his own horse examined the walls of Jerusalem, noting every section, gap, and burned-out gate. When he had no path he rode into the *wadi*, or ditch, still examining the walls. "And so I returned without the officials knowing where I had gone or what I was doing."

Nehemiah then said to the priests, the authorities, the officials, and all other responsible persons who had gathered to hear him, "You see the trouble we are in: Jerusalem is in ruins, its gates have been burned down." After presenting the facts, he enrolled them. "Come, let us rebuild the walls of Jerusalem and suffer this indignity no longer!" He also told them how the kindly favor of God had been with him, and also repeated the words of encouragement the king had given him. After his educational and inspirational appeal, the people responded, "Let us build," and with willing hands they set about the good work. (Note that the hands are willing ones. It was an Ammonite *slave* who tried to stop the enthusiastic volunteers.)

Then came Sanballat, Tobiah, and Geshem, the Arab. "They ridiculed us, and came and asked, 'What are you doing? Are you planning to revolt against the king?'" Accusations and jealousies, mixed with ridicule, are powerful tools. Thinking that perhaps the ridicule wasn't sufficient, they threw in an accusation of insubordination and treason as well.

Nehemiah answered them, "The God of heaven will give us success. We, his servants, are going to build; you have neither share nor rights nor memorial in Jerusalem. . . . God will bless us, but *we are doing the work.*" He also wisely considered the source of the accusations. These people had no interest in Jerusalem—why should he listen to them? It is important to ferret out the motives of people who accuse you. What is their stake in your failure? What do they have to lose if you succeed?

Chapter Three is an incredible recitation of the cooperation of the builders, as well as a testament to the organizational ability of Nehemiah. The list is long of the men who came to help, and my favorite words are "and next to them. . . ." It creates an awesome picture of people working together. "Joaiad and Meshullam repaired the gate of the new quarter; they constructed its framework and set doors, bolts and bars in place. *Next to them* repairs were carried out by Melatiah and Jadon . . . *next to them* repairs were carried out by Uzziel, a member of the goldsmith's guild, and *next to him* repairs were carried out by Hananiah, of the perfumers' guild . . ." (Everyone got into the work, even the perfumers' guild!) There were some problems, however, as "the chiefs of the men of Tekoah refused to bow their necks and work." Nevertheless, "The wall was soon finished all the way round to mid-height, *since the people put their hearts into the work* . . ."

"When Sanballat heard that we were rebuilding the walls he flew into a rage, beside himself with anger." He ridiculed the Jews and in front of his kinsmen and the wealthy men of Samaria he exclaimed, "What are these pathetic Jews trying to do? Do they expect to finish in one day? Do they think they can put new life into these charred stones, salvaged from the heaps of rubble?" Tobiah, that Ammonite slave, was standing beside him. "Let them build," he said, "a jackal jumping on their wall will soon knock the stones down again." Somehow Nehemiah heard these words. He prayed and said, "See, our God, how we are despised! Make their sneers fall back on their own heads." Sanballat and the others now conspired to launch an all-out attack, and upset the plans.

Nehemiah set a watch around the city, and seeing the people's fear, "I stood up and addressed the authorities, the officials, and the rest of the people, 'Do not be afraid of them. Keep your minds on the Lord, who is great and to be feared. Fight for your kinsman, your children, your wives and your homes.' Learning that we were forewarned, and that God had thwarted their plan, our enemies withdrew, and we all went back, everyone to his work on the wall."

After that Nehemiah kept only half the men working. "The rest, with spears, shields, bows and breastplates, stood behind all the House of Judah who were building the wall. The carriers, too, were armed so that each did his work with one hand while gripping his weapon with the other." You can sense the intensity of the danger in Nehemiah's following sentence. "None of us, neither myself, my kinsmen, my servants, nor the members of my personal guard, ever took off our clothes; every man kept his weapon in hand."

As is typical with so many organizations, the forces that next threatened to ruin them were internal ones. "The ordinary people and their wives began complaining loudly against their brother Jews." It seems that the officials were exacting such heavy taxes that the ordinary people complained, "We have had to borrow money on our fields and our vineyards to pay the king's tax; and though we are of the same flesh as our brothers [the officials], and our children are as good as theirs, we are having to sell our sons and daughters into slavery; some of our daughters have even been raped. We can do nothing about it, since our fields and our vineyards have been mortgaged so highly they are now the property of others."

"When I heard their complaints and their words I was very angry," wrote Nehemiah, who now had to encounter previously unseen "gaps in the wall." He held a great assembly, and reprimanded the authorities and officials. "'What a burden you impose,' I said, 'every one of you on his brother. What you are doing', I went on, 'is wrong. Do you not want to walk in the fear of our God and escape the sneers of the nations? Let us cancel this debt . . .' " The officials replied, "We will claim nothing more from them; we will do as you say." Not content to let their words go unwitnessed, Nehemiah called in the priests and made them swear to do as the officials had promised. "Then I shook out the lap of my gown with the words, 'May God do this, and shake out of his house and property any man who does not keep this promise; may he be shaken out like this and left empty!' And the whole assembly answered, 'Amen,' and gave Praise to God. And the people kept the promise."

Nehemiah used tremendous persuasive skills in his speech, reminding the errant officials of their common, and higher, goal of walking in the fear of God and "escaping the sneers of our enemies." He even used the royal "we" in saying, "Let us cancel this debt." He gave them a powerful word picture of what would happen to anyone who did not keep his promise, and once again displayed his diplomatic prowess—the same prowess that perhaps had led him to have such a great relationship with his former boss. He let everyone, even the offending parties, leave with dignity and a common goal.

He added, perhaps as evidence of his sensitivity to the financial strain the people were under, that he never even took his "per diem" allowance from them, which would have been in the form of a tax.

How much more loyalty leaders could engender in their employees if they walked the walk and talked the talk—taking a cut in their own pay, perhaps, when salaries across the board have to be reduced. There was a huge outcry from the employees of a popular airline recently when they had gone without a raise for five years, only to have their new president get a $4 million *bonus*. (I can just hear Nehemiah saying, "What you are doing is wrong," and angrily sweeping all the pencils off the table. "May you end up like splintered wood if you do not take the people's sacrifices to heart.")

When Nehemiah's enemies heard that the wall was almost complete they sent him a message: "Come and meet us in the Vale of Ono." But he replied, "I am doing a great work and cannot come down. The work would come to a halt if I left it to come to you." Four times they sent the same invitation, and he made the same reply. But the fifth message was more serious. "There is a rumor among the nations that you and the Jews are thinking of rebelling, which is why you are building the wall; that you yourself want to become their king; that you have even briefed prophets in your own interest in Jerusalem to proclaim: 'Judah has a king.' These rumors will soon be reaching the king, so you had better come and talk things over with us." Nehemiah realized "that they were trying to frighten us, thinking that our hands would tire of the work, and it will never be finished. But I meanwhile was making my hands even stronger."

Nehemiah practiced the fine art of discernment in these instances, and met their waves of veiled assault with a persistent rejoinder: "I am doing a great work and cannot come down." Like many of us, Nehemiah also had a thorn in his side. It seems that Tobiah the Ammonite slave had sworn his loyalty to Jerusalem, and began befriending a number of the city officials. These officials "even cried up his good deeds in my presence, and they reported what I said back to him." Even the most noble and well organized missions will have "leaks." Nehemiah's was no exception.

Nevertheless the walls were rebuilt *in fifty-two days*.

With the walls rebuilt, amazing things began to happen. The exiles began to return.

Nehemiah, the lover of great assemblies, summoned the people of Jerusalem. He erected a wooden dais on the Square, and asked Ezra the scribe to read and interpret the Book of the Law to all "Men, women and children old enough to understand." When the people heard the Law, they wept. Yet Nehemiah and Ezra encouraged them to rejoice in the God who loved them. "Be at ease," they were told. "This is a sacred day. Do not be sad." So the people held a great celebration.

It was this rereading of the Law, and the subsequent resolve of the people not to dishonor it again, that led to the birth of Judaism. By concentrating on a tangible deed, putting stones next to stones to rebuild a wall, Nehemiah became responsible for resurrecting the faith of an entire nation.

Nehemiah followed The Eight Action Steps to Success. Here's a quick review of his battle plan:

1. Get the facts.

Nehemiah went personally to research the situation, taking his own horse and surveying the wall during broad daylight and in the cover of darkness. He knew personally where every gap in that wall was, even though at one spot he had to crawl into a ditch to survey the damage.

2. Get a goal.

Although the burden Nehemiah felt was for the poor condition of the Jewish exiles, he determined his first and most important goal was to rebuild the wall. When he met with the people, he had a single-sentence goal: "Let us rebuild the wall."

3. Examine, educate, and enlist your resources.

Nehemiah knew each of his workers not only by their own name, but also by their fathers' names. He knew which tribes they represented, and what their particular skills were. He educated them not only about the importance of the mission, but also about the dangers they were facing. He taught them how to work with one hand and hold their weapon in the other. He enlisted them in the cause by reminding them of their common goal—to escape the sneers of the enemies.

4. Turn old business into new business.

By going back to his former employer, King Artaxerxes, Nehemiah not only got a paid leave of absence, a royal escort, and letters of recommendation, but also a promise of supplies. Had he just launched out on his own, his journey would have been much more difficult, and might not have been successful. He was among the first to "partner with his customers." It is also important to note that King

Artaxerxes was not a Jew, yet was an enthusiastic support-
er of Nehemiah's cause. Nehemiah did not look just among
his own kind, but trusted in the good will of everyone he
had encountered in the past.

5. Give them something tangible to remember you by.

Nehemiah's wisdom in building the wall first demonstrates
the principle of giving people something tangible to
remember. The visible rising of the wall as the people
worked side by side fostered a new spirit of hope and cooperation among a people who had been totally demoralized.
He also had them sign and seal their promises of reform,
knowing that a sealed document would hold more weight
than a vow spoken in celebration.

6. Break ranks. Be bold.

Nehemiah broke ranks by leaving his secure position as a
highly regarded palace attendant, forsaking the confines
of comfort to go into the wilds. He did not limit himself
to his current job description, thinking, *I am only a cupbearer.* He went from serving wine to a king to serving
hope to disheartened exiles. His boldness in asking the
king for a paid leave as well as supplies was such that he
admitted he was trembling in fear while he was doing it.
Yet he did it, and got what he requested. He boldly carried
out his strategy.

7. Get visible.

Nehemiah wrote a book about his work, which is one of the few autobiographical accounts in the Bible. Nehemiah was certain of one thing—he wanted God to remember him—and so decided to give Him "something tangible to remember him by." He also erected a dais from which the priest could read the Law—making the priest more visible, and thus what he was saying highly important.

8. Saturate all of the above with prayer.

Before Nehemiah even began his mission he wept and fasted for three days, calling upon God to give him wisdom and courage as he approached the king. At every step of his journey he called on God to help him. He began and ended his mission with a prayer, and prayed all the way through.

Questions:

1. How is your current situation like Nehemiah's? For example, are you currently employed doing one thing but feeling passionately called to do another?

2. What would you describe as being in ruins in your life, workplace, or community?

3. How can you engender the support of your

current or former boss or other powerful ally
to help you accomplish your mission?

4. How are you getting the facts about the situation? What do you realize or know about it
that others don't?

5. Have you sought deeper means of gathering
information, or have you only skimmed the
surface?

6. Who are the "exiles" or other potentially
highly interested people you might be able to
educate and enlist in helping you with your
effort?

7. How much do you know about the families
and past traditions of the people who are
working with you?

8. What forces might rise against you, and why?

9. Which of these means of trying to dissuade
and defeat you might they use?
Threats
Ridicule
False Accusations
Deceit
Infiltration
False promises

10. What *internal* problems might you encounter?
Infighting
Inequities
Bad policies from the past
Other:

11. How many "great assemblies" have you called to discuss your mission?

12. Nehemiah brought in officials, priests, and scribes. Have you alerted the same (politicians, religious leaders, reporters) regarding your mission?

13. Are you asking other people to do what you are not willing to do such as:
work late
take a pay cut

14. How are you working with one hand and keeping one hand on your weapon? Why is this necessary, and what is your weapon?

15. What will people see with their eyes when your mission is accomplished?

16. What will people feel in their hearts once your mission is accomplished?

17. Using your imagination, list four wonderful

and surprising things that could possibly occur as a result of your mission.

18. Are you proud enough about your mission to write it down on expensive parchment and present it to God?

Joan of Arc: Heeding the Call

Joan of Arc was only a child when she began to hear voices. The first time she heard a voice it simply told her, "Be a good girl. Go to church." As she grew older the voice became more instructive, and when she was in her teens the voice informed her that her mission was "to save France."

A legend had circulated throughout the country for years that a maid would save France. Joan was probably familiar with the story. But when the voice told her that she was the one whom God had chosen to free France from the grip of the English, Joan did what most of us do when we hear a prophecy or command like that—she protested. "With all due respect," she said to her "voice," "you have the wrong girl. First of all, I've never carried a spear or a lance. Second of all, women don't lead armies—they follow them. And thirdly, my father will kill me if I try to leave home on my own." All her protests were justifiable. Her father had indeed issued instructions to her brothers to kill Joan if she took out after the army, for the only women who then followed armies were prostitutes. Why he issued this prohibition is unknown. Perhaps he had a dream that she would leave. Perhaps he had noted the faraway look in her eyes. But it is definitely on record that her leaving the farm was a high-risk maneuver.

The voice then did what God is very famous for doing when issuing a call, and said, "Do what you must. But Joan, you must obey." In other words—"Here are your orders. The details are left up to you."

So Joan had two of the first eight steps in front of her. She *had a goal*— "Save France," and she *had the facts* — "The French are definitely losing." Now she applied the third step of the formula. *She examined, educated, and enlisted her resources.*

At first glance, a poor girl on a farm wouldn't seem to have many resources. She had no car, credit cards, rich parents, web site, or personal computer. She did, however, have two of the most important resources any of us can have: she had faith, and she had a friend. The friend was none other than her very own uncle, Durand Laxart. And her faith was about to become much stronger, through constant testing.

Her uncle would come to visit the farm periodically, and apparently Joan was very dear to him. On one of his visits she persuaded him to take her with him, telling him that she had a strong feeling that his wife, who was expecting a child, needed her help. The uncle made the plea to Joan's father, who let Joan go under strict orders that she would return as soon as the baby was born. On the way to her uncle's farm Joan revealed to him what her voices had told her.

In my mind I can hear the creaking of the oxcart wheels as she excitedly shared her story. I can picture her uncle cocking one ear toward her, eyes half-squinting in the sunlight and at the effort required to make sense of what she was saying.

Somehow, somewhere on that road leading away from all she knew, Joan convinced her uncle. He said "Yes, I believe you," and, more important, "Yes, I will help you." Now there were *two* believing souls.

Joan's uncle stopped in town and had Joan tell her story to his friend, a fairly successful merchant. He, also, believed, and the two of them put up the money to buy Joan a horse so she wouldn't have to walk when she went to take her plan to Charles the king, who, as yet uncrowned, was still called the dauphin.

Joan and her uncle learned where the dauphin was hiding, and knocked on the gates for three days. For three days she was told to go away. On the third day, however, the dauphin, having little else to do, decided to at least make her the occasion of some amusement. He exchanged clothes with one of the servants, and had the servant sit on the makeshift throne while he pretended to be the servant. Then Joan was summoned.

To the astonishment of all, she went straight to the dauphin even though he was hiding behind one of the pillars. She knelt at his feet and said, "God has sent me to restore you to your rightful throne." Her knowledge of who he was had to be through divine guidance, as there were no newspapers at that time, and she had never met him or even seen his picture in the tabloids. The dauphin believed her, and turned over command of his entire army to her, such as it was.

At this point Joan engaged step #4, which is: *Turn old business into new business.* The old business she had was an army—except that since they had been losing the battle with the English for so long (approximately one hundred years) they had lost their will to fight. They had no uniforms, their supplies were few, most of them hadn't been paid, and those who had been were spending it on prostitutes and gambling. Joan had to turn this old army into a new one. She had to revitalize the king's customer base.

Subconsciously or otherwise, Joan understood the next step, which is: *Give them something tangible to remember you by.* She had the French flag made up in bright colors. She was given a new set of armor which she herself polished daily. And she went out before dawn every day and roused the hung-over Frenchmen to lead them in prayer and to urge them to take confession. She banished the prostitutes, stopped the gambling, and told the army with an irresistible intensity and radiance that their mission was to free their country. Soon, they, too, believed her, and prepared to fight.

Joan had now completed the fifth step to a Successful Mission. She had *broken ranks* by casting aside the ironclad expectations of what a nice Catholic farm girl was supposed to grow up and do. She had branched out far beyond the confines of her small farm and town and was now leading armies in places that she had previously only heard about. She had *been bold* in outwitting her father and knocking three times on the king's door. And she had boiled down her mission statement into two simple words: "Save France." Joan had conquered her inner voices of doubt and fear. Yet now her external enemies began to appear.

As with any organization that has been around long enough to develop a status quo, there were certain powerful citizens of France who did not want the English to leave. They had set up cozy business arrangements with the foreigners, and stood to lose lots of money if this girl on a horse got her way.

Swearing their loyalty to the king and the country of their birth, these Frenchmen followed Joan's subsequent exploits with MRE (minimum required enthusiasm) and a much larger dose of SSI (self-serving interest). Yet, to their dismay, Joan and the newly revitalized French army began to prevail.

Praying fervently before each battle, she and the army won victory after victory. The legend began to spring up that as long as Joan was in front of them, they could not fail. And indeed, for two and a half years, it was true. She fought with the men in the swamps and the highlands, once getting knocked off her horse, only to remount it quickly and continue the rallying effort.

Her voices had told her she had three years in which to act, so she did everything with a sense of urgency and divine mission. It soon became apparent to everyone that the French were going to win. The soon-to-be king summoned his wig dresser and prepared for his coronation—an event that Joan also managed to coordinate from the battlefield, having been told by her voices as to when and where it should be. (Apparently, Joan's organizational skills knew no bounds, which is typical of many female middle-managers.)

The coronation took place with much drama and fanfare. Joan knelt before her beloved King Charles and tearfully and joyfully proclaimed her loyalty. In a rare display of generosity, he asked Joan what she would like as a gift in exchange for her service. She asked only that her uncle and his friend be repaid for the cost of her horse, and that the king no longer tax the people in her city. History books note that for the next hundred years the city of Orleans was tax exempt. In the tax rolls was the simple notation: "Taxes due: Zero. In honor of The Maid:"

The king was crowned. The French were well on their way to total victory. Yet Joan, for reasons understandable to any of us who have an ego investment in our mission, felt she had one last battle to fight. Ignoring the warnings of her inner voices, she went into battle at a town that she felt was key to sealing the victory. As she was engaging the few remaining English out in the field, French loyalists to England betrayed her, pulling up the bridge over the moat and leaving her to the mercy of her English enemies.

The English captured her and felt sure they would get a handsome ransom for her from the king. He, however, comfortable with the fit of his crown and still enjoying the partying from the coronation, said, in effect, "Joan who? Go ahead and keep her. I don't need her anymore." Anyone who had that much popularity and took such a dim view of taxation was certainly not going to find continued favor in *his* court.

Joan had shattered more than glass ceilings with her rapid rise to command she evidently broke some stained glass in the cathedrals, as well. The Catholic Church was scandalized by the fact that a pauper girl could claim to hear voices directly from heaven. The fact that she wore men's clothes and had short hair didn't sit too well with the Bishop, either. This woman had become not only a heretic but also a famous and successful one. The church decided to pay the English price on her head and bring her to trial.

The details of her trial have been made famous in many books and plays and films. "The original seventy charges against her were based mainly on the contention that her whole behavior and attitude showed blasphemous presumption; in particular, that she claimed for her pronouncements the authority of divine revelation; prophesied the future; endorsed her letters with the names of Jesus and Mary; claimed to be assured of salvation; immodestly wore men's clothing; and dared to claim that her saints spoke in French and not in English." She refused to admit that the voices she heard were from the devil. Her wit and wisdom during her trial remain a source of constant wonder, as her simple answers to difficult theological questions made fools of her inquisitors. For example, in reply to their question, "Are you in a state of grace?" she replied, "If I am not, may God put me there." When asked if she was in submission to the church proper, she replied that she knew well that the church proper could not err, but that it was to God that she held herself answerable for her words and actions.

In a weak moment, after threats of torture and

excommunication, she did recant, only to rise up even stronger the next day and proclaim that she would not and could not deny that the voices she heard were from heaven. Under this section in the trial notes are the words in French "fatal answer." The church leaders, believing that no one but they should hear heavenly voices (much less a farm girl), ordered her burned at the stake.

On May 30, 1431, the executioner seized her and led her to the stake, lighting the pyre. One of the Dominicans present, Martin Lavenu, consoled Joan, who asked him to hold high a crucifix for her to see and to shout out the assurances of salvation so loudly that she could hear him above the roar of the flames. She began to pray as the flames were lit. The executioner had never before found his task so fearful; he afterward declared that Joan's heart would not burn and that he had found it intact amid the ashes. (Encyclopedia Brittanica 200th Anniversary Edition, 1969).

The fact is that the heart of Joan of Arc remains intact to this day—inspiring each of us to look anew at what one person, with faith, can accomplish.

Joan, with her armor and her white horse and her sword and the flames, had accomplished the seventh step of her mission. *She became visible.*

And she ended her mission the same way she began it— *in prayer.*

Questions:

1. What is your still small voice telling you to do?

2. What must you overcome in order to obey it?

3. Who might be your closest friend in carrying out this mission?

4. Whom or what will you have to revitalize in order to make it happen?

5. Whom or what will you have to confront in order to get the supplies or authority you need?

6. What or who is trying to get you to deny your inner voice?

7. What kind of horse, banner, sword, and armor will you need?

8. Once your mission is accomplished, what will you ask as your reward?

Queen Esther: Timing Is Everything

Queen Esther demonstrates the importance of timing in accomplishing a mission. It seems apparent from the story of her life that she had no intentions of doing anything extraordinary. Her cousin Mordecai had adopted her upon the death of her parents, and she grew up under his watchful and loving care.

One day King Abasuerus (or Xerxes) had a royal party, in which the "drinking was unstinted," and during the festivities he commanded his queen, Vashti, to come display her beauty to his guests. For some reason, she refused, which caused the king and the officials to go into a wrath, and displace her as queen. A search went out for a suitable replacement, and the lovely Esther made the list. She was so fair in her manner and her physical presence that she soon became the King's favorite.

"Day by day Mordecai would walk about in front of the court of the harem, to learn how Esther was faring and what was to become of her." Mordecai, aware of the low esteem in which the exiled Jews were held at that time, warned Esther not to reveal her nationality or her family.

One day Haman, one of Xerxes' officials, upset because Mordecai the Jew refused to bow down to him when he passed by, informed Xerxes, "There is a certain people living apart, with laws different from those of every other people. They do not obey the laws of the king, and so it is not proper for the king to tolerate them. If it please the king, let a decree be issued to destroy them, and I will deliver ten thousand silver talents for deposit in the royal treasury." The king agreed, even handing Haman his ring to use to make the deal official. I can just hear him saying . . . "Do whatever you like. . . . Steward, bring me more wine in one of my magnificent gold cups." Thus was the doom of an entire race of people sealed.

Haman took the king's careless offer at face value, dictating an incredibly self-serving letter praising his own stature and wisdom and stating under seal of oath that all Jews were to be killed on "the thirteenth day of the twelfth month," which had been determined by casting lots.

The letter was sent to every province in Persia. "The king and Haman then sat down to feast, but the city of Susa was thrown into confusion." When Mordecai learned of the proclamation, he tore his garments and put on sackcloth and ashes. He walked through the city crying out loudly and bitterly, until he came before the royal gate, which no one clothed in sackcloth might enter.

When Queen Esther heard of this, she sent garments for Mordecai to put on, so that he might take off his sackcloth, but he refused. Instead he sent an urgent message to her through her servant: "Remember the days of your lowly estate, when you were brought up in my charge; for Haman, who is second to the king, has asked for our death. Invoke the Lord and speak to the king for us; save us from death."

Esther sent back word to him saying that it was common knowledge that anyone who went to the king without being summoned received an automatic death penalty, and she had not been summoned for thirty days.

Mordecai sent her back an intense reply: "Do not imagine that because you are in the king's palace you alone of the Jews will escape. Even if you now remain silent, relief and deliverance will come to the Jews from another source; but you and your father's house will perish. Who knows but that it was for a time like this that you obtained the royal dignity?"

Esther saw the truth in his words, and sent back the response: "Assemble the Jews who are in Susa; fast on my behalf for three days. I and my maids will also fast in the same way. Thus prepared, I will go to the king, contrary to the law. *If I perish, I perish.*"

Esther now *had the facts* and she *had a goal*: Get the King to reverse his extermination decree. She then enacted step #3: *Examine, educate, and enlist your resources.*

Esther besought the Lord God of Israel in these words:

> *My Lord, our King, the only one,*
> *come to my help, for I am alone*
> *and have no helper but you*
> *and I am about to take my life in my hands.*
>
> *I have been taught from my earliest years,*
> *in the bosom of my family,*

that you, Lord, chose Israel out of all the nations
and our ancestors out of all the people of old times
to be your heritage forever;
and that you have treated them as you promised.

But then we sinned against you,
and you handed us over to our enemies
for paying honor to their gods. Lord, you are just.

As for me, give me courage,
King of gods and master of all power.
Put persuasive words into my mouth
when I face the lion.
Change his feeling into hatred for our enemy,
that the latter and all like him
may be brought to their end.

As for ourselves, save us by your hand,
and come to my help, for I am alone and
have no one but you, Lord.
Your handmaid has not eaten at Haman's table,
nor taken pleasure in the royal banquets,
nor drunk the wine of libations.
Nor has your handmaid found pleasure
from the day of her promotion until now
except in you, Lord, God of Abraham.

O God, whose strength prevails over all,
listen to the voice of the desperate,
save us from the hand of the wicked,
and free me from my fear. 🌿

(ESTHER 4: 3–19. THE JERUSALEM BIBLE)

On the third day, when she had finished praying, she took off her suppliant's mourning attire. As she thought through her strategy she prepared to implement steps four and five. She was going to *turn old business into new business, and give the king something tangible to remember her by.*

Esther dressed herself in her full splendor. Radiant as she then appeared, she invoked God who watches over all people and saves them. Then she took two maids with her. "Having passed through door after door, she found herself in the presence of the king. When she saw the initial blush of anger in his face, she staggered, changed color, and leaned her head weakly against the maid in front of her. But God changed the king's anger to gentleness. He sprang from the throne, held her in his arms until she recovered, and comforted her with reassuring words. 'What is it, Esther? I am your brother. Take courage. You shall not die because of this general decree of ours. Come near. Speak to me.' She thanked him for his kindness, and then gave him her request. 'If it please your majesty,' Esther replied, 'come today with Haman to a banquet I have prepared.' "

The king agreed, and during the drinking of the wine said to Esther, "Whatever you ask for shall be granted, even if it is for half my kingdom.' Esther asked only that Haman and he come again the next night to a banquet that she would again prepare, and then she would make her request.

On the night of the second banquet, Esther was again asked by the king what she wanted. "If I have found favor with your majesty I ask that my life be spared, and that you spare the lives of my people, for my people and I have been delivered to destruction, slaughter, and extinction." "Who and where," said King Ahasuerus to Queen Esther, "is the man who has dared to do this?" Esther replied, "The enemy oppressing us is this wicked Haman."

The king left the banquet in anger and went into the garden of the palace, but Haman stayed to beg Queen Esther for his life, since he saw that the king had decided on his doom. When the king returned from the garden of the palace to the banquet hall, Haman had thrown himself on the couch on which Esther was reclining; and the king exclaimed, "Will he also violate the queen while she is with me in my own palace?"

Harbona, one of the eunuchs who attended the

king, apparently had little love for Haman, as he informed the king that Haman had been constructing a hanging gibbet fifty cubits high for Mordecai the Jew. The king replied, "Hang Haman instead on it." So they hanged Haman on the gibbet that he had made ready for Mordecai, and a new letter went out, releasing the Jews from their allotted destruction and urging them to defend themselves against all who attacked them.

The subsequent victory party became the Feast of Purim, as the *purr*, or lot, was cast to determine the day of their destruction. Esther remains a heroine of the Jewish people to this day, more than twenty-five hundred years after she resolved to "do the right thing, or perish."

Esther completed all eight steps to her Successful Mission. She *got the facts* about the king's evil decree from Mordecai. She *had one goal* —to reverse the decision. She *examined, educated and enlisted her resources,* calling for the prayers of others, and calling on God. She turned the *old business of a bad ruling into the new business* of having it reversed. By throwing a banquet and appearing in her royal splendor, Esther gave the King *something tangible to remember her by.* She had certainly *broken ranks*, disobeying an ill-conceived decree. She had *boldly* departed from her official duties as queen to become an advocate for social justice, boiling down her request to a simple plea: "Spare us from destruction." She literally had to *get visible* before the king in order to complete her mission, and she *soaked every one of her actions with intense and heartfelt prayer.*

Esther illustrates the importance of timing in a mission, and the fact that in more ways than we realize God may be preparing us to do something of tremendous value to others. "Who knows but that this may be why you have obtained royal dignity?" urged Mordecai, and those words are worthy of reflection for each of us in whatever position of power we currently hold. The important thing is to recognize when "our moment to act" has arrived, and, like Esther, act boldly, with honor and courage.

Questions:

1. When did you first hear of a situation that upset you enough to act?

2. What position of power do you currently hold?

3. Who are the people that you could be helping with that position or power, that you are not currently helping?

4. If you were to write a prayer to God similar to Esther's in sincerity and intensity, what would it say? Write it down here.

5. What resources are at your disposal?

6. How are you planning on timing your strategy?

Joseph: From Feast to Famine

Joseph's mission and destiny were revealed to him in two dreams that he had as a child. Twice in these dreams he saw others bowing down to him. "We were out in the field binding sheaves, and my sheaf stood up, and your sheaves all gathered around it and bowed down before it!" he told his brothers. "So you want to be our king, do you?" his brothers derided. And they hated him for the dream and for his cocky attitude. Then he had another dream and told it to his brothers. "Listen to this," he boasted. "The sun, moon, and eleven stars bowed low before me!" This time he told his father as well as his brothers, but his father rebuked him. "What is this?" he asked. "Shall I indeed, and your mother and brothers come and bow before you?" His brothers remained angry, but his father gave it quite a bit of thought and wondered what it all meant.

Joseph's sharing of those dreams, combined with his good looks and his father's obviously favoring him, led his brothers to plot his actual destruction. Planning at first to kill him, they relented at the last moment and threw him into a well. Then as they were eating supper trying to figure out what to do next, along came some Ishmaelite traders who were taking gum, spices, and herbs from Gilead to Egypt. Joseph's brothers sold him for twenty pieces of silver, and then killed a goat and spattered its blood on his coat, and took the coat to their father and asked him to identify it.

"Yes," Jacob sobbed, "it is my son's coat. A wild animal has eaten him. Joseph is without doubt torn in pieces." Then Israel tore his garments and put on sackcloth. "I will die in mourning for my son," he would say, and then break down and cry.

Meanwhile, in Egypt, the traders sold Joseph to Potiphar, an officer of the Pharaoh—the king of Egypt. Potiphar was captain of the palace guard, and the chief executioner. "The Lord greatly blessed Joseph there in the home of his master, so that everything he did succeeded." Potophar noticed this and realized that the Lord was with Joseph in a very special way. Soon he was put in charge of the administration of Potiphar's household and all of his business affairs. At once the Lord began blessing Potiphar on Joseph's behalf. All his household affairs began to run smoothly; his crops flourished and multiplied. So Potiphar gave Joseph the complete administrative responsibility over everything he owned. One day Potiphar's wife began making eyes at Joseph, who was a very handsome young man, and suggested that he sleep with her. She actually came and grabbed him by the sleeve demanding, "Sleep with me." He tore himself away, but as he did so, his jacket slipped off, and she was left holding it as he fled from the house. Potiphar's wife angrily yelled, "Rape!"

A furious Potiphar threw Joseph into prison, but the Lord was with Joseph there, too, granting him favor with the chief jailer. The jailer soon handed over the entire prison administration to Joseph, so that all the other prisoners were responsible to him. Under Joseph's guidance, everything was in order.

Pharaoh's chief baker and his wine taster fell out of favor with Pharaoh, and he had them jailed. They remained under arrest for quite some time, and Potiphar assigned Joseph to wait on them. One night each of them had a dream, but were complaining that there was no one to tell them what the dreams meant.

"Interpreting dreams is God's business," Joseph replied. "Tell me what you saw." Joseph explained the dream to each man, and his insights proved accurate. As the wine taster was leaving to return to Pharaoh's court (as Joseph had predicted), Joseph said, "Please have some pity on me and mention me to Pharaoh." Two years later when Pharaoh had a dream his magicians could not interpret, the wine taster remembered Joseph, and Joseph was summoned.

Joseph interpreted Pharaoh's dreams to mean that

Egypt would experience seven years of prosperity followed by seven years of famine. He advised Pharaoh to appoint a "director of agriculture" and divide the land into districts. Pharaoh, recognizing Joseph's gift, appointed Joseph as that person, and soon Joseph was second only to Pharaoh in authority. As Joseph predicted, famine did come, and its effects were felt back in Canaan, where Jacob, Joseph's father, and Joseph's jealous brothers lived. Things got so bad that Jacob instructed his sons to go buy grain in Egypt.

In anticipation of the famine Joseph had wisely stored excess grain during the seven years of plenty. But at last those years came to an end. Then the seven years of famine began, just as Joseph had predicted. While Egypt had sufficient grain in its storehouses, crops failed in all the surrounding countries, and their people began to starve. So now, with severe famine all over the world, Joseph opened up the storehouses and sold grain to the Egyptians and to those from other lands who came to Egypt to buy grain from Joseph.

And so it was that Jacob's sons arrived in Egypt along with many others from foreign lands to buy food. Since Joseph was governor of all Egypt, and in charge of the sale of the grain, it was to him that his brothers came, and bowed low before him, with their faces to the earth.

When Joseph saw his brothers, he did not reveal his identity to them, but pretended to think they were spies.

He sent one of them back to Canaan with instructions to return with their younger brother, Benjamin. This caused a stir among the brothers. Speaking among themselves, they said, "This has all happened because of what we did to Joseph long ago. We saw his terror and anguish and heard his pleadings, but we wouldn't listen. Now we are going to die because we murdered him."

The brothers were reluctant to have Benjamin come to Egypt, for since Joseph's "death" Benjamin had been his father's only comfort. Nevertheless, they did send one of the brothers who returned with the boy, and when Joseph saw his youngest brother, he could contain himself no longer. He dismissed the Egyptian guards from the palace and revealed his identity to his brothers. They immediately bowed in fear before him, begging him to spare their lives.

He forgave his brothers, saying, "You meant it for evil, but God meant it for good, so that I might help you and many others." Holding no malice toward them, Joseph sent the brothers back with almost more blessings than they could carry, and ordered them to bring back his father and their entire families, as there were to be five more years of famine ahead, and Joseph wanted to be able to watch over them.

They returned with an astonished Jacob, who fell upon his "once dead" son and wept for hours. Joseph caused his entire family to prosper, and continued to act as Pharaoh's ruler until he died.

With God's blessing, a lot of "humbling" time in prison, and the persistent use and exercise of his intuitive and administrative gifts, Joseph saved not only his family, but an entire civilization from death by starvation. Joseph's dream came true. (GENESIS CHAPTERS 37–50 THE LIVING BIBLE)

Questions:

1. When and how did Joseph get the facts about his mission?

2. What was Joseph's goal?

3. What resources did Joseph examine, educate, and enlist?

4. How did Joseph turn old business into new business?

5. What tangible things play a key part in Joseph's mission?

6. How did Joseph break ranks and be bold?

7. How did Joseph become visible?

8. How and when did Joseph saturate his deeds with prayer?

9. What could Joseph have done differently?

10. Was Joseph's dream part of his mission, his vision, or both?

Moses: No Great Speaker

Moses was like many people who made an impulsive attempt to accomplish a goal in their youth, and then gave it up to lead a life very far removed from their original dream. Moses, whose name means "to be drawn out," was raised in luxury in Pharaoh's palace, having been rescued from the reeds by Pharaoh's daughter. Despite the grandeur of his surroundings, Moses knew in his heart that he was a Jew, and when he was a young man he became incensed over the treatment of his kinsmen.

One day Moses went out to visit his fellow Hebrews and saw the terrible conditions they were living under. During his visit he saw an Egyptian knock a Hebrew to the ground—one of his own Hebrew brothers! Moses looked this way and that to be sure no one was watching, then killed the Egyptian and hid his body in the sand.

The next day as he was out visiting among the Hebrews again, he saw two of them fighting. "What are you doing, hitting your own Hebrew brother like that?" he said to the one in the wrong.

"And who are you?" the man demanded. "I suppose you think you are our prince and judge! And do you plan to kill me as you did that Egyptian yesterday?" When Moses realized that his deed was known, he was frightened. And sure enough, when Pharaoh heard about it he ordered Moses arrested and executed. But Moses ran away into the land of Midian. (EXODUS 2: 11–15. THE LIVING BIBLE)

The great and mighty Moses now became a shepherd following sheep. In Midian the Jewish tribes perceived him as an Egyptian, yet they nevertheless received him. He married, and had a son with his wife Zipporah, whom he named Gershom, meaning "foreigner," for he said, "I am a stranger in a foreign land."

One day as Moses was tending the flock of his father-in-law, Jethro, the priest of Midian, out at the edge of the desert near Horeb, the mountain of God, suddenly the Angel of Jehovah appeared to him as a flame of fire in a bush. When Moses saw that the bush was on fire and that it didn't burn up, he went over to investigate. Then God called out to him, "Moses! Moses! . . . Take off your shoes, for the place you are standing is holy ground. . . . I am the God of Abraham, Isaac, and Jacob. I have heard the cries of my people, and I am going to send you to lead my people out of Egypt."

After a lengthy protest, Moses was persuaded that he was the one for the mission. His main concern seemed to be that he had "a speech impediment." God agreed to give him his brother, Aaron, as a spokesman. Knowing full well the way back to Egypt, Moses now retraced the steps he had once made in haste, and went knocking on Pharaoh's door.

In a presentation that displays again the power of a boiled-down message, Moses said, "Pharaoh, the God of Israel says let my people go."

In a retort all too familiar to people who have presented a new vision to small-minded managers, Pharaoh's response was one of indignation. "Who do you think you are," Pharaoh shouted, "distracting the people from their work? Get back to your jobs!" Then, in an effort to demonstrate who was really in charge, he doubled the quota of the Jews and now gave them no straw for their bricks. This made things much worse for the Israelites. So the Israelites came to Moses (their God-chosen leader) and swore at him. "May God judge you for making us stink before Pharaoh and his people," they said, "and for giving them an excuse to kill us."

Moses, in a pattern that was to become familiar, went back to his boss for a new set of instructions. However, God said, "When I am through with Pharaoh, he will not only let my people go, he will drive them out." When Moses told the people what God had said, they would no longer listen, for they were too dispirited after the tragic consequence of his previous message. So Moses went back again, and this time God decided to give Pharaoh something tangible to remember Him by. Rivers turned into blood, frogs began hopping around inside the palace, flies began swarming relentlessly around Pharaoh himself, and Pharaoh's livestock were destroyed.

Pharaoh relented briefly after each calamity, saying, "Yes, the people may go," but after each plague ended he would reverse his previous ruling. Finally, God sent out an angel of death to kill all the first-born male Egyptians. Losing his son brought Pharaoh to his knees, and at last he let God's people go.

If Moses had simply accomplished this much, he might have felt his mission was complete. Although Moses' mission was to free the Israelites from the slavery of Egypt, he had also been given the mission of delivering them to the promised land.

The journey Moses then undertook has been made famous through thousands of years of retelling. He led his people across the Red Sea, carved out the Ten Commandments, set up judicial law, and put up with a lot of grumbling. He taught and guided the people for another forty years. Before his death he was led up to the mountain overlooking Canaan, and shown the valley where the people were to be ultimately settled.

The man whose name meant "to draw out" had fulfilled his mission, drawing his people out of the land of slavery and leading them to the land of promise.

In accomplishing his mission, Moses also employed the eight action steps.

He *had the facts* about life in Egypt, having seen it from the very balconies of the palace. He also knew the deserts leading away from Egypt intimately, having lived there, as well. He *had a goal*, which was the freedom of the Israelites. He *examined, enlisted, and educated his resources*, meeting at length with the Jewish elders and telling them of his plans before he met with Pharaoh. He practiced turning his rod into a snake before he threw it down in front of Pharaoh. And with an incredible series of miracles, Moses certainly *gave people something tangible to remember him by*. By reliving his dream of freeing the Israelites, *he turned old business into new business*—this time acting under God's guidance to accomplish his mission. He *broke ranks and was bold*, risking his life on numerous occasions as he challenged the almighty Pharaoh with only a wooden staff. And, *he got visible*. Whether he was coming down from the mountains carrying the Ten Commandments or appearing in the palace just as Pharaoh was piling up dead frogs, Moses never missed a dramatic opportunity to "show up." He *saturated everything he did with prayer* and was known, in fact, as "the man who talked with God."

Moses offers us other examples, as well. He proved you can never be too old to take on a bold and mighty mission. When he had his momentous encounter with God in the desert, he demonstrated for all of us that *wherever* we are standing is holy ground. God's power is not limited to palaces or marble halls. In going back to Pharaoh as many times as necessary, he showed that persistence is as important an ingredient as miracles in getting things done. Moses did not rely on appearances to justify his obedience, for as he was in the process of freeing the Israelites, things actually temporarily got worse for them, rather than better. He listened to God, and believed God, and was not swayed by his drop in the opinion polls.

Moses proves that God never forgets our dreams, even when *we* seem to have forgotten them. God would not have chosen this humble man to set the Israelites free if He had not seen that very ember of a dream glowing in Moses' heart, even though Moses had the dream of justice for the Israelites when he was only a youth. He did not get called to act on it until nearly sixty years later.

And Moses also demonstrates that once you have a vision, you can never feel quite at home no matter where you are. Once you have seen that vision, either in the desert or high up on a mountain, you can never really take your ease again. The vision you see will be like "the bush that never consumes itself, even as it burns."

Questions:

1. What is your "speech impediment?"

2. What injustice causes you to go into a rage?

3. How many times are you willing to "go back to Pharaoh" in order to get the deed done?

4. Do you believe God could combine *your* upbringing, experience and passion to accomplish something great?

5. Where are you standing right now?

Ruth

Of the sixty-six titles that comprise the Old and New Testaments, only two are named after women—Esther and Ruth. Given the fact that women were then so rarely esteemed, the fact that Ruth was not a Jew but a Moabite from a formerly "cursed, heathen tribe" makes it all the more remarkable that she was included in the written and oral traditions of the patriarchal Israelites.

The story of Ruth bears inclusion in this book about finding one's path because her mission was simply to love, and be present, for another human being. As she gave of herself without measure, her mission began to unfold.

"Once in the time of the judges," a man named

Elimelech left Bethlehem because of a famine and moved to the land of Moab. While there, he and his wife Naomi bore two sons, who in turn married girls of Moab—Orpah and Ruth. But later, all three men died, so that Naomi was left alone without her husband or sons. Both daughters-in-law planned to return with her to Jerusalem, but she told them, "It is better for you to return to your own people." Grieving that she had neither husband nor sons now to help them, Naomi said, "Oh, how I grieve for you that the Lord has punished me in a way that injures you."

And they cried together, and Orpah kissed her mother-in-law good-bye, and returned to her childhood home, but Ruth insisted on staying with Naomi. "See," Naomi said to her, "your sister-in-law has gone back to her people and to her gods; you should do the same."

With tears in her eyes, Ruth made this appeal:

> *Do not press me to leave you*
> *and to turn back from your company,*
> *for wherever you go, I will go.*
> *Wherever you live, I will live.*
> *Your people shall be my people,*
> *and your God shall be my God.*
> *Wherever you die, I will die*
> *and there I will be buried.*

May Yahweh do this thing to me and more also,
if even death should come between us! 🌿
(RUTH 1: 16–18. THE JERUSALEM BIBLE.)

Seeing that she was determined to go with her,
Naomi said no more. Upon returning to Jerusalem Naomi
told people, "Don't call me Naomi (which means Pleasant)
any longer, but call me Mara (which means bitter)—for
Almighty God has dealt me bitter blows. I went out full
and the Lord has brought me home empty; why should you
call me Naomi when the Lord has turned his back on me
and sent such calamity!" (Naomi demonstrates that she
had seen her "role" as wife and mother as her mission.
When those roles changed, she went into a depression—
not seeing the blessing God had right at hand, which was
Ruth.)

"And they came to Bethlehem at the beginning of
the barley harvest." Many times when you feel at your low-
est, the harvest is just beginning. Ruth, who apparently was
not only loyal but entrepreneurial, said, "Perhaps I can go
out into the fields of some kind man to glean the free grain
behind his reapers." And Naomi replied, "All right, dear
daughter. Go ahead." Ruth, simply thinking of what she
could do to make her mother-in-law's life better, ended up
"by coincidence" in the fields of Boaz, who was a wealthy

relative of Naomi's husband. Boaz arrived from the city while she was working diligently in the fields. After exchanging greetings with the reapers he asked his foreman, "Who is that girl over there?" And the foreman replied, "It's that girl from the land of Moab who came back with Naomi. She asked me this morning if she could pick up the grains dropped by the reapers and she has been at it ever since." Boaz went over and talked to her. "Listen, my child," he said to her. "Stay right here with us to glean. Don't think of going to any other fields. Stay right behind my women workers; I have warned the young men not to bother you; when you are thirsty, go and help yourself to the water." She thanked him warmly. "How can you be so kind to me?" she asked. "You must know I am only a foreigner."

"Yes, I know," Boaz replied, "and I also know about all the love and kindness you have shown your mother-in-law since the death of your husband, and how you left your father and mother in your own land and have come here to live among strangers. May the Lord God of Israel, under whose wings you have come to take refuge, bless you for it." "Oh, thank you, sir," she replied. "You are so good to me, and I'm not even one of your workers." Boaz not only gave her extra food for lunch, but he also instructed his reapers to deliberately snap off some of the heads of barley and drop them for her to glean.

Seeing the generous leftovers, and the barley, Naomi began to perk up. "Praise the Lord for a man like that! God has continued his kindness to us as well as to your dead husband!" Naomi cried excitedly. "Why, that man is one of our closest relatives!" She instructed Ruth to go lay at his feet, and when he awoke to find her there, Ruth asked him to marry her. "Make me your wife according to God's law, for you are my close relative."

Boaz, being an honorable man, squared things with a relative in town who by law would have had first rights to marry Ruth. The man gave his permission, and Boaz and Ruth were married.

Ruth and Boaz had a child, and Naomi was blessed once again. The women of the city said to Naomi (in what was to be a positive prophecy), "'Bless the Lord who has given you this little grandson. May he be famous in Israel. May he restore your youth and take care of you in your old age, for he is the son of your daughter-in-law who loves you so much, who has been kinder to you than seven sons!' And they named him Obed. He was the father of Jesse and grandfather of David, King of Israel." (BOOK OF RUTH, CHAPTERS 1–4. THE LIVING BIBLE.)

Ruth completed the eight steps to mission fulfillment in the following ways. When Ruth looked into her heart and recognized the love she had for Naomi, she *had all the facts* she needed. She *set a goal*, and it was this: to be with and bless Naomi. She *examined and enlisted her resources* by looking around at the ripe barley fields, and asking if she could labor there.

She *turned old business into new business* by invoking an ancient law—proposing to Boaz and bringing to his awareness a law that was perhaps dusty on the books but was now staring him in the face through the eyes of this intense young woman. Boaz was eager to marry her because *she had given him something tangible to remember her by*—her diligent work in the fields, as well as her reputation for loving-kindness and loyalty. Ruth definitely *broke ranks* by leaving her Moabite roots and homeland to follow Naomi, and *her boldness* was apparent in that she refused to turn back when Naomi first asked her to, even though her sister-in-law obeyed.

Ruth *became visible* by working out in the fields, and bringing about a face-to-face meeting with the person whose blessing she sought. She *saturated everything she did with prayer* —invoking the blessing of a God she knew only through Naomi.

Ruth demonstrates to all of us the value of the ministry of presence, and the worth God places on loyalty and commitment. Ruth's words to Naomi are used in wedding ceremonies still—thousands of years after she spoke them. She did not change any geographical boundaries or turn water into blood or lead people into the promised land. She simply loved someone with all her heart, and gave herself in service. It is no wonder that she was chosen to be Jesus' ancestor. God must have wanted that kind of passionate love for others to be handed down.

Questions:

1. How devoted are you to the people God has placed in your life?

2. How do you measure that devotion?

3. Are you willing to leave *your* comfort zone to make them more comfortable?

4. Are you looking at every possible way you can serve them, working diligently in the field as well as speaking words on a hill?

5. Do you know what your inheritance rights are? Do you know what theirs are?

6. Do you feel you can only "belong" to someone if you are related by blood?

7. If you knew someone had a blessing that you needed, would you be willing to go lie at their feet until they noticed you?

Pitfalls and Potholes

It would be hazardous to assume that because you now have a clearly articulated mission and vision statement, you can consider yourself home free. Proverbs warns, "If you intend to serve the Lord (and follow a high calling), prepare yourself for an ordeal."

Wisdom offers a keen study of the mistakes of others, and those who know history need not repeat it.

Following are examples of pitfalls and potholes that these famous leaders encountered as they sought—and sometimes failed—to stay on The Path. This section may be the closest thing to a "hazard zone" map that I can provide, with shortcuts and detours clearly laid out that others have successfully followed. If we can be alert to the already clearly marked dangers on the road, we will know in advance how to negotiate our way through them or, better yet, to avoid them altogether.

Pitfall and Pothole Number 1:
Feelings of Inadequacy

You've been given a mission and now you're telling God, or thinking to yourself, "This job is too big for me." This pothole is perhaps one of the biggest on the path, because if you do not get over it, you will never even be able to step on the road at all. Many leaders have found this to be the first obstacle they encountered. See if you can match these quotes to the individual who cried, muttered, or stuttered them. Put a check mark by any that match your current feelings.

1. "I am no great speaker." (I'd rather die than speak in front of an audience.)

2. "I am the least of my house." (Surely you can find someone better.)

3. "I am too young to be a prophet." (I am not age qualified.)

4. "I am a person of unclean lips." (If you only knew my past . . .)

Answers: 1. Moses, 2. King Saul, 3. Jeremiah, 4. Isaiah

Moses and the Speech Impediment

When Moses was told by God that he was the one to utter the words "let my people go," Moses replied, *"But, Lord, I'm just not a good speaker. I never have been, and I'm not now, even after you have spoken to me, for I have a speech impediment!"*

God told Moses, "Who makes mouths? . . . I will help you to speak well, and I will tell you what to say. And since you insist, I'll also send along your brother Aaron to help you." (EXODUS 4: 10–14. THE LIVING BIBLE)

Saul of the Least Family

When Samuel the prophet told a young Saul that he was destined for the wealth of Israel, Saul replied, "Are you kidding? I am a Benjamite—the smallest of Israel's tribes. And *my family is the least of all the families of the tribe of Benjamin!"*

Nevertheless, Samuel anointed Saul King of Israel. (I SAMUEL 9:21–27.)

Jeremiah: Too Young to Speak

One day the Lord said to Jeremiah, "I knew you before you were formed within your mother's womb; before you were born I sanctified you and appointed you as my spokesman to the world." Jeremiah's reply to this was, *"O Lord God, I can't do that! I am far too young! I am only a youth!"*

"Don't say that," God replied, "for you will go wherever I send you and speak whatever I tell you to. And don't be afraid of the people, for I, the Lord, will be with you and see you through." Then he touched my mouth and said, "See, I have put my words in your mouth. Today your work begins . . ." (JEREMIAH 1: 4–10. THE LIVING BIBLE)

Isaiah—the Foul-Mouthed Sinner

In the year that King Uzziah died Isaiah saw the Lord. "He was sitting on a lofty throne, and the temple was filled with his glory." This vision upset Isaiah tremendously, and he said, "My doom is sealed, for *I am a foul-mouthed sinner, a member of a sinful, foul-mouthed race, and I have looked at the king.*"

Then one of the seraphs flew over to the altar and with a pair of tongs picked out a burning coal. He touched my lips with it and said, "Now you are pronounced not guilty because this coal has touched your lips. Your sins are forgiven." Then Isaiah heard the Lord asking, "Whom shall I send as a messenger to my people? Who will go? And Isaiah said, "Lord, I'll go! Send me." (ISAIAH 6:1–8. THE LIVING BIBLE)

Questions:

1. Do you feel inadequate to do the mission you've been assigned? If so, why? List all your reasons here.

2. What do you think God's reply to you about each of these "inadequacies" would be?

Pitfall and Pothole Number 2:
Accusations of Others

You're moving along, accomplishing your task and feeling pretty good about things, until you read a critical review of your efforts in the newspapers, or hear about them at a board meeting, or overhear them in the lunchroom. Others, too, have had the same problems. Who said these words?

1. "Why did you leave the sheep to come down here? Go back home, you show-off!"

2. "Who set you up as our leader anyway?"

3. "You aren't from God, you are from the devil."

Answers: 1. David's brothers, 2. the Israelites addressing Moses, 3. the Scribes and Pharisees addressing Jesus

David and His Brothers

When David went down to take his brothers lunch, he discovered the Israelites trembling in their tents, shuddering at the threats of the Philistine Goliath. David started saying that somebody ought to take this giant on, and restore the dignity of Israel. But when David's oldest brother, Eliab, heard David talking like that, he was angry. *"What are you doing around here, anyway?" he demanded. "What about the sheep you're supposed to be taking care of? I know what a cocky brat you are; you just want to see the battle!"*

But David persisted . . . "When I am watching sheep, if a lion or bear comes and grabs a lamb from the flock, I go after it . . . I have killed both lions and bears, and I'll do it to this heathen Philistine, too, for he has defied the armies of the living God! The Lord who saved me from the claws and teeth of the lion and the bear will save me from Goliath!" As Goliath approached, David ran out to meet him and, reaching into his shepherd's bag, took out a stone, hurled it from his sling, and Goliath fell on his face to the ground. (I SAMUEL 18: 28–50. THE LIVING BIBLE)

Moses and His Doubters

One day Miriam and Aaron were criticizing Moses, and they said, *"Has the Lord spoken only through Moses? Hasn't he spoken through us, too?"*

The Lord heard them. Immediately He summoned

Moses, Aaron, and Miriam to the Tabernacle. "Come here, you three," He commanded. . . . So they stood before the Lord. (Now Moses was the humblest man on earth.) . . . And the anger of the Lord grew hot against Miriam and Aaron. He departed . . . And Aaron cried out to Moses, "Oh, sir, do not punish us for this sin; we were fools to do such a thing!" (NUMBERS 12: 1–9. THE LIVING BIBLE)

Jesus and the Scribes and Pharisees

"*You Samaritan! Foreigner! Devil!*" the Jewish leaders snarled. "Didn't we say all along you were possessed by a demon?"

"No," Jesus said, "I have no demon in me. For I honor my Father—and you dishonor me. And though I have no wish to make myself great, there is One who decides true greatness." (JOHN 8:48. THE LIVING BIBLE.)

Questions:

1. What accusations, internal or external, have been, could be, or probably will be hurled at you regarding your mission?

2. What tools do you have in your "shepherd's bag" that have given you victory in small ways before? What would happen if, like David, you had more faith in:

a. your aim, and

b. God's protection?

3. Which family members or close associates might be trying to stop you on your mission?

4. Who is ultimately the determiner of your mission, and your greatness?

Pitfall and Pothole Number 3:
The Small-Mindedness of Others

As a leader you are charged with seeing the big picture, and looking out for the best interests of everyone in your charge. Even the best team members will have days when they doubt you, and the mission, and begin to complain about the blisters on their hands or feet. Who also had to listen to whining like this?

1. "We are tired of eating manna. At least they fed us well in Egypt."

2. "The ordinary people and their wives began complaining."

3. "Who will get to sit next to you on the throne?"

Answers: 1. Moses, 2. Nehemiah, 3. Jesus

Moses and the Complainers

Then the Egyptians who had come with them began to long for the good things of Egypt. This added to the discontent of the people of Israel and they wept, "Oh, for a few bites of meat! Oh, that we had some of the delicious fish we enjoyed so much in Egypt, and the wonderful cucumbers and melons, leeks, onions, and garlic. But now our strength is gone, and *day after day we have to face this manna!"*

"Tell the people to purify themselves, for tomorrow they shall have meat to eat. . . . And the Lord sent a wind that brought quail from the sea, and as far as one could walk in a day in any direction, there were quail flying three or four feet above the ground." (NUMBERS 11:4–6, 18, 31. THE LIVING BIBLE)

Nehemiah and the Complaints of the Ordinary People

About this time *there was a great outcry of protest* from parents against some of the rich Jews who were profiteering on them. Families who ran out of money for food had to sell their children or mortgage their fields, vineyards, and homes to these rich men, and some of them couldn't even do that, for they had already borrowed to the limit to pay their taxes.

"I was very angry when I heard this, so after thinking about it I spoke out against these rich government officials. 'What is this you are doing?' I demanded. 'How dare you demand a mortgage as a condition for helping another Israelite?' Then I called a public trial to deal with them . . . and I pressed further. 'What you are doing is very evil,' I explained. 'I beg you, gentlemen, stop this business of usury. Restore their fields, vineyards, olive yards, and homes to them this very day and drop all your claims against them.' So they agreed to do it." (NEHEMIAH 5: 1–13. THE LIVING BIBLE.)

Jesus and the Power-Hungry Staff Members
Then the disciples began to argue among themselves as to who would have the highest rank in the coming Kingdom.

"The one who serves you most will be your leader," Jesus replied. (LUKE 22: 24–26. THE LIVING BIBLE)

Questions:

1. What complaints are you hearing?

2. Which of them are based on:
   a. false memories of how good things were before you came along
   b. legitimate concerns
   c. a desire for power and recognition?

Pitfall and Pothole Number 4: Distraction

Rather than being defeated by all out attacks, too many of us never accomplish our missions simply because we get distracted. Which of these people had these distractions?

1. "But his heart was misled by many wives."

2. "But his heart was tied to his riches."

3. "Come down off that wall. We have some important things to tell you."

Answers: 1. Solomon, 2. the rich young man, 3. Nehemiah

Solomon and His Many Wives

King Solomon married many other women besides the Egyptian princess. Many of them came from nations where idols were worshipped—even though the Lord had clearly instructed his people not to marry into those nations . . . lest they start worshipping other gods. *Yet Solomon did it anyway.*

Jehovah was very angry with Solomon about this, for now Solomon was no longer interested in the Lord God of Israel. So now the Lord said to him, "Since you have not kept our agreement and not obeyed my laws, *I will tear the kingdom away from you and your family and give it to someone else.*" (1 Kings 11:1–12. The Living Bible)

Jesus and the Rich Young Man

Once a Jewish religious leader asked Jesus this question: "Good sir, what shall I do to get to heaven?" Jesus told him to obey the ten commandments. The man replied, "I've obeyed every one of these laws since I was a small child." "There is still one thing you lack," Jesus said. "Sell all you have and give the money to the poor—it will become treasure for you in heaven—and come, follow me." But *when the man heard this he went sadly away, for he was very rich.*

Jesus watched him go and then said to his disciples, "How hard it is for the rich to enter the Kingdom of God! It is easier for a camel to go through the eye of a needle than for a rich man to enter the Kingdom of God." (Matthew 19:24)

Nehemiah and the False Invitation

"When Sanballat, Tobiah, Geshem, and the rest of our enemies found out that we had almost completed the rebuilding of the wall—though we had not yet hung all the doors of the gates—they sent a message asking me to meet them in one of the villages. But I realized they were plotting to kill me . . . *Four times they sent the same message, and four times I gave the same reply.*

I replied, 'I am doing a great work! Why should I stop the work to come and visit with you?'" (Nᴇʜᴇᴍɪᴀʜ 6:1–4. Tʜᴇ Lɪᴠɪɴɢ Bɪʙʟᴇ)

Questions:

1. How many idols are you worshipping?

2. What "riches" may be keeping you from heaven?

3. What distracting invitations have you been receiving?

4. What will be your reply?

5. How many times are you able to say no to persistent temptations?

Pitfall and Pothole Number 5: Fear

If you are afraid, you may never act. Fear is always present when you undertake a great cause. These leaders felt the fear, but were undaunted.

1. "What if the king kills me?"

2. "What if Pharaoh doesn't believe me?"

3. "My heart was pounding as I raised the question to the King."

1. Queen Esther, 2. Moses, 3. Nehemiah

Esther, the Brave Queen

Esther knew that if she went in to approach the king without being summoned, she would automatically be put to death. It was the law. This knowledge caused so much fear in her that she almost refused the mission. Nevertheless, "On the third day, when she had finished praying, she dressed herself in her full splendor. She invoked God who watches over all people and saves them. Then she took two maids with her. With a delicate air she leaned on one, while the other accompanied her, carrying her train. *She leaned on the maid's arm as though languidly, but in fact it was because her body was too weak to support her.* Rosy with the full flush of her beauty, *her face radiated joy and love; but her heart shrank with fear.* Having passed through door after door, she found herself in the presence of the king."

Consequence:

The king, noticing the color draining from her face, sprang from the throne and said, *"What is the matter, Esther? Take heart; you will not die;* our order only applies to ordinary people. Come to me." (ESTHER 5: 1–14. THE JERUSALEM BIBLE)

Moses the Fearful Leader

Moses was so afraid of facing the Egyptians that he initially fled the country. Later, when told he was the one who must not only return to Egypt but confront the same Pharaoh who had ordered his execution, *Moses invoked his speech impediment as a reason not to go.*

Nevertheless, he went, along with Aaron, his brother with the willing voice. "*So Moses and Aaron did as the Lord commanded them.*" (EXODUS CHAPTER 4: 10–13 AND CHAPTER 7:20. THE LIVING BIBLE)

Nehemiah, Working with Sword in Hand

A man who works with his sword in his hand and doesn't sleep much at night is not a man without fear. *Nehemiah's heart trembled as he approached the king* with his initial request for a leave of absence, and he was daily aware of the dangers that faced him as he undertook his mission.

Nevertheless, "the work *was completed in fifty-two days.*" (NEHEMIAH 1–6 THE LIVING BIBLE)

Questions:

1. Write down all your fears. Write till you can write no more.

2. Now write down what you imagine (or know) God's responses to each of these fears would be.

Pitfall and Pothole Number 6: Impatience

One of the challenges of completing a mission successfully is having the patience to see it through to its full completion. These people wanted to hurry things along. Who were they?

1. "Maybe if I kill an Egyptian."

2. "If the priest doesn't show up in fifteen minutes."

3. "Lord, shall we just annihilate them right now?"

Answers: 1. Moses, 2. Saul, 3. James and John

Moses and His Temper

Moses was among the greatest leaders of all time. Yet, he had a temper, and a tendency towards impatience. Remeber, he killed an Egyptian in a fit of anger about the way the Jews were being treated. (EXODUS 2: 11–15. THE LIVING BIBLE)

Consequence:

Moses ended up in exile, herding sheep, for more than forty years.

Saul, the Impatient King

Samuel had told Saul earlier to wait seven days for his arrival, but when he still didn't come, and his troops were rapidly slipping away, Saul decided to sacrifice the burnt offering and the peace offering himself. But just as he was finishing, Samuel arrived. Saul went out to meet him and to receive his blessing, but Samuel said, "What is this you have done?" Saul made some excuse, saying, "Well, when I saw that my men were scattering from me, and that you hadn't arrived by the time you said you would, and that the Philistines were at Michmash, ready for battle, I said, 'The Philistines are ready to march against us and I haven't even asked for the Lord's help!' *So I reluctantly offered the burnt offering without waiting for you to arrive.*"

Consequence:

"You fool!" Samuel exclaimed. "You have disobeyed the commandment of the Lord your God. He was planning to make you and your descendants kings of Israel forever, but now your dynasty must end, for the Lord wants a man who will obey him." (1 SAMUEL 13:8–14. THE LIVING BIBLE)

James and John, the Pyromaniacs

One day Jesus sent messengers ahead to reserve rooms for them in a Samaritan village. But they were turned away!

The people of the village refused to have anything to do with them because they were headed for Jerusalem. When word came back of what had happened, James and John said to Jesus, *"Master, shall we order fire down from heaven to burn them up?"*

But Jesus turned and rebuked them, saying, "You don't realize what your hearts are like. For the Son of Man has not come to destroy men's lives, but to save them." (LUKE 9: 52–56. THE LIVING BIBLE)

Questions:

1. What task or process are you being tempted to hurry along?

2. When do you feel tempted to do so?

3. What could be the possible consequences of your "rush to glory?"

Pitfall and Pothole Number 7: Compromise
Although every mission involves a host of negotiations, you will occasionally be tempted to make a compromise that is unwise, and only serves to dilute or defeat your ultimate purpose. This leader struck a compromise that did not prove to be beneficial.

Hezekiah, the Hesitant King

In the year 701 B.C., Hezekiah had reigned as king of Jerusalem for fourteen years. Only twenty-five years old when he first became king, and "he did what is pleasing to Yahweh." Almost immediately "he abolished the high places, broke the pillars, cut down the sacred poles and smashed the bronze serpent that Moses had made; for up to that time the Israelites had offered sacrifice to it; it was called Nehushtan. He put his trust in the God of Israel. And so Yahweh was with him, and he was successful in all that he undertook."

However, for some reason, Hezekiah grew more fearful the longer he sat on his throne. When Sennacherib, king of Assyria, attacked the fortified towns of Judah and captured them, Hezekiah king of Judah sent this message to the king of Assyria at Lachish, "*I have been at fault. Call off the attack, and I will submit myself to whatever you impose on me.*" The king of Assyria then demanded a settlement of 300 talents of silver and 30 talents of gold. Hezekiah gave him all the silver in the temple of Yahweh and all the gold in the treasury of the royal palace. "He even stripped the gold facing from the leaves and jambs of the doors of the temple, and gave it to the king of Assyria."

Evidently, Hezekiah wanted peace at any price. Nevertheless, the king of Assyria sent his men to demand a meeting with Hezekiah. "They demanded that King Hezekiah come out to speak to them, but instead he sent a truce delegation of the following men: Eliakam, his business manager; Shebnah, his secretary; and Joah, his royal historian." The Assyrian ambassador proceeded to hurl threats and insults to the entire city, even though the truce delegation begged him, "Please speak in Aramaic, for we understand it. Don't use Hebrew, for the people standing on the walls will hear you."

Consequence:

Despite having received and accepted Hezekiah's "settlement offer," *the Assyrian king was not satisfied.* His ambassador replied, "Has my master sent me to speak only to you and to your master? Hasn't he sent me to the people on the walls, too? For they are doomed with you to eat their own excrement and drink their own urine!" (When Hezekiah had allowed himself and God's temple to be humiliated, how could the humiliation of the entire nation not be far behind?)

It was only *after* the truce delegation came back with this message to Hezekiah that he went into the temple to pray. It was only *then* that he sought out Isaiah, the prophet, as well. Isaiah replied that the Lord had heard the Assyrian insults. "The Lord says, 'Tell your master not to be troubled by the sneers these Assyrians have made against me.' For the king of Assyria will receive bad news from home and will decide to return; and the Lord will see to it that he is killed when he arrives there." The prophecy did indeed come true, and the Assyrians were beaten back through divine intervention, *not* through a compromise based on fear. (2 KINGS 18–19. THE LIVING BIBLE.)

Questions:

    1. What compromise are you about to make based on fear?

    2. Have you sought God's help and answer *first* on this matter?

    3. Which situation in recent history is reminiscent of this passage in 2 Kings, where modern leaders tried to appease an evil ruler's appetite?

    4. What were the results of that compromise?

Pitfall and Pothole Number 8: Apathy

There will be times when the sun seems too hot and the workers' bellies are so full and there are so many other interesting things for them to do that apathy will be your biggest obstacle. These leaders also stared into apathy's dull eyes. Who were they?

1. "Why are your boats still sitting in the harbor?"

2. "I've taken off my shoes, am I to put them on again?"

1. Deborah, 2. Song of Solomon

Deborah, the Bold Leader

The one who was responsible for bringing the people back to God was Deborah, a prophetess. One day she summoned Barak and said to him, "The Lord God of Israel has commanded you to mobilize ten thousand men to fight King Jabin's mighty army . . ." Barak replied, "I'll go, but only if you go with me!" When Barak summoned the men of Zebulun and Naphtali to mobilize at Kedesh, ten thousand men volunteered, and Deborah marched with them . . . The enemy was defeated. . . .*But the tribe of Reuben didn't go. Why did you sit at home among the sheepfolds,"* Deborah lamented, *"playing your shepherd pipes? . . . Why did Gilead remain across the Jordan . . . why did Dan remain with his ships? And why did Asher sit unmoved upon the seashore, at ease beside his harbors?*

"But the tribes of Zebulum and Naphtali dared to

die upon the fields of battle. The very stars of heaven fought Sisera . . . Praise the Lord," Deborah sang. "Israel's leaders bravely led, the people gladly followed! . . . *How I rejoice in the leaders of Israel who offered themselves so willingly . . . May those who love the Lord shine as the sun!*" And after that there was peace in the land for forty years. (JUDGES 4–6. THE LIVING BIBLE)

Consequence:
The apathetic tribes were listed by name as those who did not help the Lord or Israel.

The lazy bride

One night as I was sleeping, my heart awakened in a dream. I heard the voice of my beloved; he was knocking at my bedroom door. "Open to me, my darling, my lover," he said, "for I have been out in the night and am covered with dew." But I said "*I have disrobed. Shall I get dressed again? I have washed my feet, and should I get them soiled?*" My beloved tried to unlatch the door and my heart was moved for him. I jumped up to open it, but he was gone . . .

Consequence:
The bride then had to go searching for him in the streets, not only

getting her feet soiled, but getting beaten up in the process.
(SONG OF SOLOMON 5: 2–8. THE LIVING BIBLE)

Questions:

1. Where have you encountered apathy about
   the mission?
   —In yourself?
   —In others?

2. What are the possible consequences to those
   (including you) who might be apathetic
   towards your mission?

Pitfall and Pothole Number 9: Pride

As your mission becomes more and more successful you
may be tempted to take more credit than you deserve. The
following people in scriptures let pride fill their hearts, and
it turned out to be a snare to each of them.

1. "Well, if you really want to honor me . . ."

2. "He died because he got hung up on his hair."

3. "Look at the kingdom which I have built.
   Was it not built by me alone?"

Gideon and His "One Request"

The entire story of Gideon bears rereading, because here was someone who was so afraid of trouble that he spent his days hiding in a wine vat. Nevertheless, in what proved to be a positive prophecy, the Angel of the Lord appeared to him and said, "Mighty soldier, the Lord is with you!" The Angel commissioned him to raise an army against the Midianites. Gideon was convinced of his calling only after he requested and received three miraculous signs from heaven, two of which involved laying out a fleece.

Finally, however, Gideon was convinced, and he raised the army. He instructed them to do as he did, and when the trumpets sounded, to shout, *"We fight for God and for Gideon!"* (This is the first clue to the pride in his heart. Can you imagine Moses saying, "Let the people go—for God and for Moses!") Well, God works even with fleeces, wet or dry, and Gideon and his army prevailed. The success was so profound, in fact, that after it was over, "The men of Israel said to Gideon, 'Be our king! For you have saved us from Midian.' Gideon replied, 'I will not be your king . . . the Lord is your King. However, I have one request. Bring me all your gold and jewelry . . .'" Gideon personally took this gold, made an ephod or symbol out of it, and took it to his home town.

Consequence:

"But all Israel soon began worshipping it, so it became an evil deed that Gideon had done." (EXCERPTS FROM JUDGES 7–9. THE LIVING BIBLE)

Absalom and His Hair

Now no one in Israel was such a handsome specimen of manhood as Absalom, and no one else received such praise. He cut his hair only once a year—and then only because it weighed three pounds and was too much of a load to carry around.

Absalom rose up in rebellion against his own father, King David, and wrought much heartache and trouble wherever he went. His goal was to wear his father's crown, and to steal his kingdom from him. He was so convinced of his worth and beauty that *he even built a monument to himself in the King's Valley, calling it, appropriately enough, Absalom's Monument.*

However, one day in the forest of Ephraim a battle began between his troops and David's men. The battle raged all across the countryside, and more men disappeared in the forest than were killed. During the battle Absalom came upon some of David's men, and as he fled on his mule, it went beneath the thick boughs of a great oak tree, and *his hair caught in the branches.* His mule went on, leaving him dangling in the air.

Consequence:

Joab, his sworn enemy, disobeyed the king's command not to harm Absalom should he be captured. He took three daggers and plunged them into the heart of Absalom as he dangled alive from the oak . . . *hanging by his beautiful hair.* Ten of Joab's young armor bearers then surrounded Absalom and finished him off. (2 SAMUEL 14: 25 AND 18: 6–18. THE LIVING BIBLE)

Nebuchadnezzer and His Unwilling "Veggie Diet."

Nebuchadnezzer was a very proud king who loved to, among other things, erect golden statues of himself that were ninety feet high and nine feet wide. Anyone who wouldn't bow down to these statues was tossed into a furnace. The prophet Daniel interpreted a strange dream of Nebuchadnezzer as meaning that God was not pleased with his prideful ways, but the king refused to change.

Twelve months after this dream, he was strolling on the roof of the royal palace in Babylon, saying, *"I, by my own mighty power, have built this beautiful city as my royal residence, and as the capital of my empire."*

While he was still speaking these words, a voice called down from heaven, "Oh King Nebuchadnezzar, this message is for you: You are no longer ruler of this kingdom. You will be forced out of the palace to live with the animals in the fields, and to eat grass like the cows for seven years until you finally realize that God parcels out the kingdoms of men and gives them to anyone he chooses."

Consequence:

"That very same hour the prophecy was fulfilled. Nebuchadnezzar was chased from his palace and ate grass like the cows . . . until seven years later he looked up to heaven, and his sanity returned." (DANIEL, 4. THE LIVING BIBLE)

Questions:

1. What "one request" of your followers could you make that might prove a snare to you?

2. What point of pride do you have that could, literally, become your "hang up?"

3. What are you thinking that you have done, and done well, "alone and by your own power?"

4. What monuments to yourself are you building?

❧ Echoes of Champions ❧

As much as each of the individuals in the preceding section are worthy of admiration, we do both ourselves and them a disservice if we "pedestalize" them or see them as being more than the flesh and blood that they were. They were given to us as examples so that we might learn from them and also rise to the same heights of courage and accomplishment.

In this section I intend to prove that you have more in common with these champions than you realize. If that is indeed so, you also have the same potential, ability, and responsibility to follow and fulfill your highest calling. Please answer the following questions:

Like Nehemiah:	yes	no
I like my current job.	_____	_____
I always inquire about:		
—foreign affairs	_____	_____
—others' welfare	_____	_____
I trust and respect my current boss.	_____	_____
I'm not afraid to ask for help in bold and specific ways.	_____	_____

Recently, I heard something that made me weep. It was: _____

_____

I know something needs to be rebuilt.	_____	_____

	yes	no

I have examined my task from
every possible angle.   _____   _____

I have gathered information about
my mission in the following ways: _____

_____

_____

_____

I have a list of the people who are
willing to help me.   _____   _____

I know their names, and their
family members' names.   _____   _____

I know what their highest gifts are,
and their special training.   _____   _____

I know that I am doing a great work. _____   _____

I have enlisted, enrolled, involved, and
informed:
— Officials (politicians)   _____   _____
— Scribes (reporters)   _____   _____
— Priests (religious leaders)
in and about my work.   _____   _____

I know what my opposition will be.   _____   _____

I know that this is what they are saying about me: _____

_____

_____

My response to them is: _____

_____

_____

I work with one weapon in my hand at all times. It is this:

_____

_____

I want to be remembered for: ——————————————————

————————————————————————————————————.

❧ Echoes of Champions ❧

Like Joan of Arc: yes   no

I sometimes hear voices.   _____   _____
I've always felt a little different.   _____   _____

My family is /will be/ has been opposed
to my mission. (circle one)

I have no formal training for
what I'm about to do.   _____   _____

	yes	*no*

I feel _____ too young
_____ too ignorant
_____ too ill-equipped to handle
this job.

I have shared my mission with
a friend.   _____   _____

I have been given what I need
at each step of my journey.   _____   _____

I use the power of prayer.   _____   _____

I am a great motivator.   _____   _____

I hate to see people not
using their gifts.   _____   _____

I love to see people on
their rightful throne.   _____   _____

I have knocked on the doors of kings.   _____   _____

I am not afraid of confrontation.   _____   _____

I believe God can use anyone to
accomplish great things.   _____   _____

I am willing to relocate.   _____   _____

I am willing to change costumes.   _____   _____

	yes	no
I only visualize and work toward positive outcomes.	_____	_____
I hear the sounds of battle all around me, even now.	_____	_____

I saw no unusual future for myself, until _____

_____

_____ .

	yes	no
I am not concerned with issues of gender if God isn't.	_____	_____
I will obey my inner voice no matter what the cost.	_____	_____

❧ Echoes of Champions ❧

Like Joseph:	yes	no
I have had dreams of greatness.	_____	_____
I have had encounters with jealous "family" members.	_____	_____
I know how much my real Father (in heaven) loves me.	_____	_____
I have been tempted.	_____	_____

	yes	no

I know what it feels like to be thrown into a pit of despair. _____ _____

I know what my special gifts are. _____ _____

I use my gifts to help others at every opportunity. _____ _____

I do a good job for everyone I serve. _____ _____

Some people think I have died already. _____ _____

I have learned or am learning skills far from my home. _____ _____

I know I will face my accusers again. _____ _____

When I do, I will say to them: _____

_____

_____

When I do, I will give them ————————————————

_____

_____

I take the time to listen to my dreams. _____ _____

I take the time to listen to the dreams of others. _____ _____

	yes	no

I use my gifts even when
I'm in the pits.   _____   _____

My enemies tried to harm me, but God turned it to good
in the following ways: _____

_____

_____

I have been given powerful
opportunities to help others.   _____   _____

The greatest of these opportunities is _____

_____

_____

✤ Echoes of Champions ✤

Like Esther: *yes*   *no*

I am in favor with the
powers that be.   _____   _____

Few people know my true identity.   _____   _____

I am living or working in a place that
is not my natural environment.   _____   _____

	yes	*no*
I have a mentor or loving and watchful guide like Mordecai.	_____	_____
I am mostly unaware of larger issues outside my palace walls.	_____	_____
I am very aware of the internal modus operandi, "To do/To *not* do."	_____	_____
I am on the Best-Dressed list.	_____	_____
I know the power of fragrances, real and imagined.	_____	_____
I am aware that sequential requests can be more powerful than "dumped" ones.	_____	_____
I have tact, subtlety, and a strategy.	_____	_____

If I step out and do what must be done, the following will/could happen

• to me _____

• to others _____

If I do not step out, the following will/could happen

• to me _____

• to others _____

I have been given a special power to help others.	_____	_____

Like Moses:	*yes*	*no*
I sometimes have a temper.	_____	_____
I often act impulsively.	_____	_____
I am doing a job far below what my early and original training called for.	_____	_____
I feel like I eat sheep dust all day long.	_____	_____
My shoes are getting worn thin from going over the same ground.	_____	_____
I'm getting too old to do anything new.	_____	_____
I tried once to accomplish my mission, but it didn't work out.	_____	_____
Nobody ever listens to me.	_____	_____
I feel like I don't belong here.	_____	_____
I was raised in a culturally diverse setting.	_____	_____
I am surrounded by ungrateful complainers.	_____	_____
My work is at times very monotonous.	_____	_____

	yes	*no*

I've been accused of trying to do
too much. _____ _____

I saw something I'll never forget. I made
a deep impression on me. It was ————————————

_____

_____.

If I only had _____, then I would
be powerful.

I disappear into the clouds at times,
causing people to wonder if I'm
coming back. _____ _____

I am angered by injustices, especially these:_____

_____

_____.

I like to come up with logical steps to
help people with their problems. _____ _____

I look at other people like _____ and _____ and think
"Now they could really do something about _____."

I am aware that God may call me to return to _____.

This makes me feel _____

_____

	yes	no
In the past when I've tried to make things better for people, it only got worse.	_____	_____
I am humble.	_____	_____
People say I talk to God.	_____	_____

I want the following people freed: _____

_____

_____

	yes	no
I hate to get my feet wet.	_____	_____
I believe that God does what God says.	_____	_____
I am willing to risk my neck for what I believe.	_____	_____
I know that I am authorized to work miracles.	_____	_____
I use my staff to work wonders.	_____	_____

I am standing overlooking a valley, feeling a sense of
anticipation and hope for the future. In the valley I see:

_____

_____

_____

Like Ruth: yes   no

I feel it is important to "be there"
for others.   _____ _____

I've suffered losses in relationships
before.   _____ _____

Some people say I have an unusual sense of kindness
toward _____.

No job is too small or demeaning
for me.   _____ _____

I think it's important to make verbal
commitments, and keep them.   _____ _____

I trust everything will turn out right
as long as love is in my heart.   _____ _____

I am aware of my rights.   _____ _____

I am aware of my legal inheritance.   _____ _____

I am willing to venture into
the unknown.   _____ _____

I believe service is the highest calling
a person can have.   _____ _____

I believe that the "ministry of presence"
is as important as any I could have.   _____ _____

I have a reputation for loyalty
and kindness.   _____ _____

I am not concerned with previous
negative curses which have been placed
on me and "my kind of people."   _____ _____

When I love someone, I hold
nothing back.   _____ _____

I am aware that true love may
cause me to leave my comfort zone.   _____ _____

I prove my dedication through hard
work.   _____ _____

I believe that even a small act of kindness
will have repercussions for generations.   _____ _____

Give yourself one point for every *yes* answer, two points for every blank you filled in on the essay questions, and zero points for every *no* answer. Total your score for each section.

If your total score equals 12 or more, you are on the path to being a champion.

CASE HISTORY: PERSONAL

I have always felt it to be somewhat dishonest for authors to write instructional guides for others without including some personal revelation about their own experience with the process they are espousing. Like Jonas Salk, if I believe my vaccine will work, then I should be willing to inject it into my own veins. Although my story may be far less inspirational or illuminating than those of the people I've presented, I want to confirm to you that I am endeavoring to live these principles in my own flesh.

I knew two things from the time I was five years old: One, that I wanted to own horses, and two, that after watching every episode of *Gunsmoke*, I didn't want Miss Kitty's job—I wanted Marshal Dillon's.

I was fascinated with cowboys and tales of the Wild

West. A friend of mine who used to help my mother car-pool recalls picking me up for school one day when I was about seven. I was dressed in a cowboy hat, cowboy pants, boots, and vest, and I had a holster on. "Laurie, you look so cute!" she exclaimed. "Is it dress-up day at school?" I looked up at her with a solemn face and said, "No," as I quietly climbed into her car.

When people would ask me what I wanted to be when I grew up I would say, "I'm going to have a horse ranch," and they would smile. By the time I was ten I was writing poems and hiding them under my bed. In response to people's questions about my future I began to say, "I am going to have a horse ranch, and be a writer."

I grew up, got married, got educated, got divorced (or "freed" as I like to call it). In the meantime I decided that I wanted to own my own business, and at the same time deliver a message of God's love to others.

When I met my boss Catherine at the Women's Resource Center, I was divorced and poorer than a church mouse, but I had a dream that I could use my skills and talents to help people. I had decided that I should become a social worker (which I realized later was my father's dream for his unlived life). Catherine helped me focus on my true talents, and after observing me spend all my off-work time at the racquetball club or looking at sports cars, she convinced me that I probably was not cut out to be someone helping poor people downtown. I felt unmasked the day she called me into her office and delivered this observation. "But how could I be a Christian and not help poor people?" I asked her. She replied, "Not all poverty is financial. God made you who you are. Live out your talents and your gifts, and you'll help God the most. The best thing you can do for anybody is to be a good example." That began our search for my new career.

Catherine said, "You are a natural born promoter. And you love art. Maybe there's something you can do that would combine the two." Thus was born my ad agency. I began taking new client calls at lunch—keeping my day job at the Y—and when I realized that I could earn more as a $20-per-hour consultant than as a $4.00-per-hour YWCA worker, I made the leap. I still have in my files the letter I wrote to Jesus, dedicating my new company to Him and his work, volunteering to be "an ad agency for God." That was in 1980.

Once the agency became successful in El Paso, I decided to branch out into San Diego. I turned over my Texas agency to a manager and headed west. This impulsive decision led to a total loss of clients in El Paso. So much for my first attempt at bilocation.

The San Diego agency was soon successful, however. I began to invest in real estate, thinking that real estate would offer me retirement income, and allow me to eventually—oh, yeah—write for God. Properties were appreciating at 22 percent a year. I began buying houses and refinancing them to buy other houses, and took on a partner who had similar business interests. When it became apparent that she had incredible administrative abilities, I asked her to help me with the ad agency, as well.

Soon, we were at the point where we needed more capital if we were to expand, and that's when I met a businessman from New York whose stated goals were to "Hit a home run and help the world while doing so." He also offered to help.

My new partners and I went on a two-day retreat and emerged with this as our mission statement:

"To recognize, promote, and inspire divine excellence in ourselves and others."

This became our working document and guiding light. We had it cast in metal and mounted on the corporate mantel to remind us how to conduct ourselves.

What we did not realize was how powerful a mission statement can be, and how it could transcend the borders and boundaries we had so neatly in mind. This particular mission statement became a living thing. It lifted us up by its claws like an eagle and carried us to distant cliffs. The ride was exhilarating, the view, frightening. And suddenly it seemed that we were no longer in control.

We had painstakingly developed an eight-page

action plan with print so tiny you had to read it with a magnifying glass. We even brought in a specialist to illustrate it with graphs and charts. I proudly showed it to Catherine, who declared, "Laurie, this looks like a recipe for a heart attack. There's no way you can do all those things!" Unfortunately, I ignored her. Everything looked so good on paper, and our projections seemed so realistic and exciting, that we would stay up all hours into the night, planning our success. The "plan" was to hire and train a staff that could replace me, while we expanded the agency from a local to a nationally renowned marketing firm specializing in health care. Then, with the profits thrown off from this efficient and finely tuned organization, I could "buy my time to write."

That was the plan. Suddenly, however, I found that the only thing I wanted to do was write a book about Jesus. Now! My partners, well aware of my long-time dreams and wanting to help me accomplish them, cautiously suggested that we build the ad agency first, and use the profits to buy my "time out."

I wish I could say that this happened. It did not. As the months passed I became like an agitated, pregnant race horse, pacing and snorting and wanting to lie down and give birth to this thing inside me—despite the colors I was wearing and the trainer and fans who were counting on me to run. I became impatient and irritable. I found the staff we had hired for the expansion to be well-meaning people who nonetheless increased my burden with their questions and need for training. I would attempt to make marketing calls, only to find myself secretly hoping that we wouldn't get the account, knowing that each new account would only give me less time to write the book that was churning inside me.

To make matters worse, real estate in California suddenly reversed its seemingly endless upward spiral, and the investment properties that were supposed to generate cash flow for the agency began making giant sucking sounds. The bank, which had for the previous four years automatically rolled over a line of credit I had, went into its own panic due to the California recession, and called all unsecured loans due. My New York partner stepped in and wired the money, yet that drained half of our allotted development funds. The two top-notch sales people we hired made hundreds of cold calls, only to come up—cold. The money for the ad agency expansion was going quickly, and in ways that didn't seem to make sense. It was during this time that I came across a passage in scripture that spoke directly to me.

"Is this a time for you to live in your paneled houses, when my House lies in ruins? So now, Yahweh Sabaoth says this: Reflect carefully how things have

gone for you. You have sown much and harvested little; you eat but never have enough, drink but never have your fill, put on clothes but do not feel warm. The wage earner gets his wages only to put them in a purse riddled with holes. So go to the hill country, fetch wood, and rebuild my House: I shall then take pleasure in it, and be glorified there, says Yahweh.

"Yahweh Sabaoth says this: Reflect carefully how things have gone for you. The abundance you expected proved to be little. When you brought the harvest in, my breath spoiled it. And why? It is Yahweh Sabaoth who speaks. Because while my House lies in ruins you are busy with your own, each of you. That is why the sky has withheld the rain and the earth withheld its yield. I have called down drought on land and hills, on wheat and new wine, on oil and on all the produce of the ground, on man and beast and all their labors. . . . But take courage now. Courage, all you people . . . It is Yahweh who speaks. To work! I am with you—and my spirit remains among you. Do not be afraid! For Yahweh Sabaoth says this: A little while now, and I am going to shake the heavens and the earth, the sea and the dry land. I will shake all the nations and the treasures of all the nations shall flow in, and I will fill this Temple with glory, says Yahweh Sabaoth.

"Mine is the silver, mine the gold! The new glory of this Temple is going to surpass the old, and in this place I will give peace." ❧

(HAGGAI CHAPTERS 1: 4–11 AND 2: 4–9.
THE JERUSALEM BIBLE)

I read that passage, and it was as if the wind had been knocked out of me. Despite my best intentions to use my real estate profits to help me do God's work, I was making so much money so quickly that it "only made sense" to buy more real estate and make more profits. And the ad agency I had once dedicated to God had become so profitable that "it only made sense" to expand it and make more profits. So there I was, living in my paneled house, neglecting God's.

I knew then I had to write that book about Jesus, no matter what it cost. I began to spend weekends at a desert place called Gold Rock Ranch where there was no phone, and no distractions, and just write. Friends would join me in the evenings, but the daytime was devoted to me and that computer.

And as I was writing the strangest thing began to happen. A sense of peace enveloped me. It felt like a warm mist, full of sunshine. And when I was sitting at the computer writing, it sometimes felt as if I was actually nursing a child.

I came back with a manuscript that my partners read

and said, "This could be a best seller." Nevertheless, they felt that my major efforts should still be toward the ad agency. My heart sank, because I knew it wasn't in me anymore. At least not now. The Jones Group would not, at this rate, become the huge health care ad agency we had envisioned. Our development funds were by now exhausted. All our "plans" had collapsed. I remember one day, after a solemn review of our bottom line, looking over at our silent metal mission statement on the mantel, and thinking, "What have you done to us?"

Yet in my heart of hearts I knew that writing *Jesus, CEO* was absolutely, totally in line with our mission statement, even if it didn't relate to building an ad agency. And I also knew that if I didn't do it, something in me would die.

I eventually bought both partners out, which left me with a minimally functioning ad agency, four properties that were worth less than I owed on them, and buy-out agreements that showed me nearly two hundred thousand dollars in debt. I remember sitting with an accountant as he was totaling up all the debt I had accumulated. He said, "Laurie, this is really serious. Why are you looking so happy?" The only explanation I had was that I knew now that I was on the right path, and it didn't matter what it had cost me to get there.

During the transition year following the publication of *Jesus, CEO*, I was led to Dee Jones, an incredible administrator who now handles all of my business affairs. I have since purchased a horse ranch "so big it covers two states." (Actually, it is a lovely horse property that happens to have the New Mexico–Texas state line running right through the corrals. But when you are a Texan, you have to talk big. It's expected.)

Thanks to the success of *Jesus, CEO*, the negotiating ability of my agent, Julie Castiglia, and the faith of Bob Miller, president of Hyperion, I received a significant advance for my next two books. ("Mine the silver, mine the gold" . . . God promised in Haggai.) I am now living the dream I had when I was ten years old—which was to "have a horse ranch and be a writer."

I am still diligently working on carrying out my mission. With Catherine constantly challenging me to ask myself, "What does 'divine excellence' actually, really mean?" I have now refined my former mission statement, and changed the words "divine excellence" to "divine connection." My updated mission statement is:

"To recognize, promote and inspire
the divine connection
in myself and others."

I have begun a foundation with the profits of *Jesus, CEO* whose mission statement is the same.

When I'm not writing, consulting, or giving seminars, I am wearing a cowboy hat, jeans, boots and looking at horses. *Now*, every day for me is dress-up day. Just like it ought to be.

🌿 *"Under his eyes I have found true peace."*
Song of Solomon 8: 10 🌿

🌿　　　🌿　　　🌿

A vision statement I have chosen to study is taken directly from a passage in scripture. I have found no other to be so challenging or beautiful. I ask you to ponder with me its beauty and its meaning. Perhaps it can be a vision statement for us all.

THE SPRING IN THE TEMPLE
He brought me back to the entrance of the Temple,
where a stream came out from under the Temple
threshold and flowed eastward . . . The man went to
the east holding his measuring line and measured off a
thousand cubits; he then made me wade across the
stream; the water reached my ankles. He measured
off another thousand and made me wade across the

stream again; the water reached my knees. He measured off another thousand and made me wade across again; the water reached my waist. He measured off another thousand; it was now a river which I could not cross; the stream had swollen and was now deep water, a river impossible to cross.

He then said, "Do you see this?"

He took me further, then brought me back to the bank of the river. When I got back, there were many trees on each bank of the river. He said, "This water flows east down to the Arabah and to the sea; and flowing into the sea it makes its waters wholesome.

Wherever the river flows, all living creatures teeming in it will live. Fish will be very plentiful, for wherever the water goes it brings health, and life teems wherever the river flows.

There will be fishermen on its banks. Fishing nets will be spread from En-gedi to En-eglaim. The fish will be as varied and as plentiful as the fish of the Great Sea.

The marshes and lagoons, however, will not become wholesome, but will remain as salt.

Along the river, on either bank, will grow every kind

of fruit tree with leaves that never wither and fruit that
never fails; they will bear new fruit every month,
because the water comes from the sanctuary. And
their fruit will be for food and their leaves for
healing." ⚘

(EZEKIEL 47: 1–12)

Although I may never fully comprehend the symbolism or imagery here, several things are very clear to me. The water comes from the temple, which is the place of worship. The water becomes more wholesome as it searches for the sea, its larger "oneness." Some of the water will never reach the sea, but will become marshes and lagoons. Nevertheless, even this water will be left for something useful—salt. The river will grow, naturally and immeasurably. There will be varied, plentiful fish, and many workers will earn their living from this water. Trees of different kinds grow all along both banks of the river. The fruit is to be used for food, and the leaves for healing.

My responsibility is to make sure that the water of my life springs from the temple—a place of worship, and flows ever outward—always reaching toward the sea.

MEDITATIONS

Wake up,
Wake up,
and clothe yourself with strength.
Put on your beautiful clothes.
Rise from the dust,
take off the slave bands from your neck . . .
. . . recognize that it is I, yes, I, who speaks to
[you]. ✣

ISAIAH 52: 1–2, 6. (THE LIVING BIBLE)

Feed the hungry! Help those in trouble! Then your
light will shine out from the darkness and the darkness
around you shall be as bright as day.

*And the Lord will guide you continually, and satisfy
you with all good things, and keep you healthy too;
and you will be like a well-watered garden, like an
ever flowing spring. Your children will rebuild the
long-deserted ruins . . . You will be known as "The
People Who Rebuild Their Walls and Cities."* ✺

ISAIAH 58: 10–12 (THE LIVING BIBLE)

*In all you do, be the master. And·do not spoil the
honor that is rightly yours.* ✺

ECCLESIASTICUS 33:23. (THE JERUSALEM BIBLE)

*For I am the Lord your God, the Lord of Hosts, who
dried a path for you right through the sea, between the
roaring waves. And I have put my words in your
mouth and hidden you safe within my hand. I planted
the stars in place and molded all the earth. I am the
one who says, "You are mine."* ✺

(ISAIAH 51: 14–16. THE LIVING BIBLE)

Conclusion

As you began this book I asked you to sit, take three deep breaths, and say to the world

> I see you, World.
> I see your beauty.
> And I sense your pain.
> And I am here for you.

In closing I ask you to visualize the God of all creation looking directly at you, and saying

> I see you, _____.
> I see your beauty.
> And I know your pain.
> And I am here for you.

Acknowledgments

My agent Julie Castiglia and Bob Miller, my publisher, gave this project life and breath when it was merely an idea. Rick Kot, my editor, kept me going with his hilarious memos about Louise, his talking parrot, and allowed me to infuse humor into this rather serious subject. David Cashion, his assistant, handled all details of the manuscript efficiently and with apparent joy. Carol Perfumo and the entire Publicity Department helped get the word out. Dee Jones, my administrator, kept my world in order during the writing of this book, and continues to provide invaluable structure and support. (Dee also came up with all the verbs on pages 50–57. Good work!)

I want to thank David Whyte for bringing poetry back into the soul of corporate America, Robert Fritz for putting his observations on creativity into words, and Catherine Calhoun for her ongoing inspiration and feedback. She is in many ways my compass and my guide.

This year I gained incredible insight and inspiration from working with the leaders of St. Joseph's Hospital, Cardone Industries, First Presbyterian Church in Orlando, and the Gorbachev Foundation. These people are forging new ways of delivering service to humankind.

Thanks especially to my mother, Irene Jones, who this year suffered a silent heart attack while sneezing, emerged from angioplasty with stories that had the entire cardiovascular unit laughing, and who so nearly left us but has so clearly graced us with more time. She has taught me more than anyone that there are only two paths worth walking—the first and most important one being The Spiritual Path, and the second and more mundane one being any path that leads to a mall.

And mostly I want to thank God for leading me, feeding me, and heeding me. The promise of the Lord proves true.

Gift Offer

Dear Reader,

If you would like a free bookmark that has the Eight Action Steps printed on it, please send us your name and mailing address, and enclose a self-addressed stamped #10 (11–inch long) envelope. For every name and stamped, self-addressed envelope that you include, we will enclose a complimentary bookmark.

Please send all requests to:

Dee Jones

The Jones Group

813 Summersong Court

Encinitas, Ca. 92024

Fax (760) 634-2707

laurie@lauriebethjones.com

For information on speaking engagements, or consulting work, please call Dee toll free at 1-888-JESUSCEO (1-888-537-8723) or at (760) 753-7251, 9 A.M. to 5 P.M. California (Pacific) time. You may also reach us through our web site at www.lauriebethjones.com

Thank you so much for your interest and support. I look forward to seeing you ON THE PATH.

Sincerely,
Laurie Beth Jones

Index

Aaron, 157, 174, 175, 183

Abasureus, King (Xerxes), 141–42, 146

Absalom, 194–95

Absenteeism, xii

Accidents, 19–20

Accusations of others, 173–76
   questions about, 175–76

Action plan, and key words, 64

Age, and mission, 160, 170, 171–72

Aglow (magazine), 16

American Express corporation, xiv

"A mission must be full of suffering" assumption, 15–16

Amos, Wally, 45

Apathy, 189–92
   questions about, 192

Apollo 13 (film), 93–94

Artaxerxes, King of Persia, 115, 116–17, 126–27

Asking for help, 108

Barak, 190

Benjamin, 153

Big picture, 23–25

Boaz, 163–65

Boldness, 110–11

Book of Ruth, 165

"Break ranks. Be bold" action step, 110–11
   and Joan of Arc, 135
   and Moses, 159, 160
   and Nehemiah, 127
   and Queen Esther, 147
   and Ruth, 166

Business plan, 106

Calhoun, Catherine, 12
Cancer Society, 17
Career
   as mission assumption,
     9
   mission statement as insur-
     ance for, xvii
   parallel or shadowing
     dream, 18–19
Career counselors, xv
Catholic Church, 137–38
Champions, finding echoes of,
   196–209
Champy, James, x, 77
Change, 31
   and vision of future,
     77
Charles, King of France
   "Dauphin," 133–34,
   136–37
Chevy trucks
   and self–image, 26–27
Childhood
   exercise, 43–44
   and USP, 42
Children, as mission, 11
Clarity, 76
Columbus, Christopher,
   71–72
Commitment, x, 166–67

Companies
   change, and vision, 77
   and employees' mission
     statements, 68–69
   recruiting, 87
   vision statement of, 87
Compromise, 186–89
   questions about, 189
Conscious creating, 80–81
Contacts, 108–9
Control, 66
Cooperation, 119–20
Core value or cause, 58
Corinthians, 31
Corporations
   CEOs, xiv
   writing mission statement
     for, xv
Cousteau, Jacques, 15
Covey, Stephen, x, xiv–xv,
   11–12
Cowan, Dave, 76
Creative tension zone, 93–100
   action steps for getting
     through, 103–14
   defined, 96, 97
   exercise, 98–100
   and success, 98
"Cup of pain or sorrow" exer-
   cise, 37–38

Daniel, 196
David, King of Israel, 165,
    173, 194
    and Goliath, 174, 175
Death, 11
Deborah, 190–91
Decision-making, xvii
Depression, 11
Descriptive details, 74
Despair, xiii
Distraction, 179–81
    questions about, 181
Divine excellence, 222
Divinely ordained mission, 15
    vs. economically or cultur-
        ally ordained mission,
        26
Divorce
    and downsizing, xiii
    and role as mission, 11
Downsizing, xii–xiii
Dreams, 149

Ecclesiasticus, 230
Eight action steps to success,
    103–14
    break ranks, be bold,
        110–11, 127, 135, 147,
        159, 166

examine, educate, and
    enlist your resources,
    106–9, 126, 132, 143,
    147, 159, 166
get the facts, 103–5, 125,
    132, 143, 147, 159, 165
get a goal, 105–6, 126, 132,
    143, 147, 159, 165–66
get visible, 111–12, 128,
    139, 147–48, 159, 166
give them something tan-
    gible to remember you
    by, 109–10, 127, 128,
    134, 145–46, 147, 159,
    166
saturate everything you do
    with prayer, 112–14,
    128, 136, 139, 145, 148,
    159, 166
turn old business into new
    business, 108–9, 126,
    134, 145, 147, 159, 166
Einstein, Albert, 90
Eliab, 174
Eliakam, 188
Elimelech, 162
Employee's mission statement,
    69
Employer (boss)
    how to talk to, 117, 129

Employer (boss) (*cont.*)
    mission statement of, 68–69
"Empty nest syndrome," 11
Enthusiasm, 49
Environment, 106
"Escape velocity," 77
Esther, Queen, 105, 140–49
    and fear, 182
    finding echoes of, 203–4
    questions about, 148–49
Esther, 145
"Examine, educate., and enlist
    your resources" step,
    106–9
    and Joan of Arc, 132–33
    and Moses, 159
    and Nehemiah, 126
    and Queen Esther, 143–45,
    147
    and Ruth, 166
Exodus, 156, 171
Ezekiel, 225
Ezra, the scribe, 125

Family expectations, 33–38
    exercise, 37–38
    power of positive, 38
"Famous Amos Cookies "
    and sharing a gift, 45

Fear, 181–83
    number one, x
    questions about, 183
Feelings of inadequacy,
    170–73
    questions about, 173
Finances, 107
Fortune, xiii
"For whom" element, 58–60
"Four elements" exercise,
    27–29, 31–32
Friends, 107
Fritz, Robert, 78, 94, 95, 97–98
Frost, Robert, 25
Future, creating, 72–73

Gedalia, 59, 75–76
Genesis, 25, 154
"Geography is destiny"
    assumption, 17–18
Gershom, 156
Geshem, 119, 180
"Get a goal" step, 105–6
    and Joan of Arc, 132
    and Moses, 159
    and Nehemiah, 126
    and Queen Esther, 143,
    147
    and Ruth, 165–66

"Get the facts" step, 103–5
  and Joan of Arc, 132
  and Moses, 159
  and Nehemiah, 125
  and Queen Esther, 143, 147
  and Ruth, 165
"Get visible" step, 111–12
  and Joan of Arc, 139
  and Moses, 159
  and Nehemiah, 128
  and Queen Esther, 147–48
  and Ruth, 166
Gideon, 193–94
Gifts and talents
  exercise to find, 46–47
  looking at—today, 44 47
  as resources, 106
"Give them something tangible to remember you by" step, 109–10
  and Joan of Arc, 134–35
  and Moses, 159
  and Nehemiah, 127, 128
  and Queen Esther, 145–46, 147
  and Ruth, 166
Goals, 105–6. See also "Get a goal" step
Goliath, 174

Governments, xii
Gravitational pull, 76–77
"Great assemblies," 130
Groups/ causes list, 60–63

Haman, 141–42, 146–47
Hammer, Michael, x, 77
Hanaiah, 120
Hanani, 115
Harbona, 146–47
"Hazard zone" map, 169
Healing, 14
Health, 107
Heart Aroused, The (Whyte), 15
Hezekiah, King of Judah, 187–89
Hobbies, 106, 107
Hospital administrators, xiv
How to Argue and Win Every Time (Spence), 87
Human rights, 13–14

"I am not currently living my mission" assumption, 12–13
"I am not important enough to have a mission" assumption, 13–14

I Could Do Anything—If I Could Only Figure Out What I Want (Shur), 33

Identity
   changing, 31
   and job, 9–10
   and role, 11
Imagination, 90
Impatience, 184–86
   questions about, 186
Internal problems, 130
"Inventory" of resources, 106
Isaiah, 172, 188–89
Isaiah, 229, 230
It's a Wonderful Life (film), 13

Jabin, King, 190
Jacob, 150, 153–54
Jadon, 120
James, 113
James, William, 80
James and John, and impatience, 184, 185–86
JAZZERCISE, 42
Jeremiah, 171–72
Jesus
   and accusations of others, 173, 175

and being specific, 75, 80
and childhood, 43
"for whom" of, 58–59
and James and John; the pyromaniacs, 185–86
mission statement of, xi, 15, 65
and prayer, 113–14
and rich young man, 180
and self-knowledge, 26
and small-mindedness of others, 176, 178
on talent, 45–46
vision statement of, 86–87
Jesus, CEO, xv, 110, 221–23
Jethro, 156
Joab, 195
Joah, 188
Joaiad, 120
Joan of Arc, 4, 131–40
   finding echoes of, 199–201
   heart of, 139
   questions about, 140
   trial of, 138–39
Job
   leaving, 117
   as mission assumption, 9–10
   and mission statement, 65–68

vs. personal mission state-
ment, xvii
Job, 113–14
Joseph, 109, 149–55
    finding echoes of, 201–3
    questions about, 154–55
Judges, 191, 194
Jung, Carl, 34

Kersee, Jackie Joyner, 38
Key action words or verbs
    developing action plan
        from, 64–65
    exercise, 58–59
Kings, 180, 189
Knowing yourself, 26–27
    four elements exercise for,
        27–29
    word picture exercise for,
        29–30
Knowledge base, 105

Labor problems, xii
Landscape, effect of, on mis-
    sion, 18
Lavenu, Martin, 139
Laxart, Durand, 132–33
Lazy bride, 191–92

Leaders, 12–13
Leider, Richard, x
"Life is random. Even I was an
    accident" assumption,
    19–20
"Like a rock" slogan, 26–27
Lincoln, Abraham, 3
Loosening the mind, 24
Loyalty, 166
Luke, 178, 186

Managers, and downsizing,
    xii–xiii
Mandela, Nelson, 3–4
Marketing and advertising,
    106–7
Marriage, vision statement for,
    82–86
Material wealth, 106
Matthew, 15, 45, 46, 113, 180
Meaningless life, x
Means of trying to dissuade
    and defeat, 129
Meditation
    and big picture, 23–25
    four elements exercise,
        27–29, 31–32
    inspiration for, 229–30,
        231

Meditation (*cont.*)
    on "randomness" of life,
        21–22
    word picture exercise,
        29–30
Melatiah, 120
Merton, Thomas, 12
Meshullam, 120
Michelangelo, 98
Mindful presence, 24
Mind maps, 74
Minimum required enthusiasm
    (MRE), 136
Ministry of presence, 166
Miriam, 174, 175
Missett, Judy, 42
Mission
    effect of, on others, 130–31
        enlisting resources in,
        106–7
    forgetting, 6–7
    vs. goal, 105–6
    how to form sense of, 23–32
    how to fulfill, xviii, 101–69
    and Joan of Arc, 131–40
    and Joseph, 149–55
    and Moses, 155–61
    and Nehemiah, 115–30
    pride in, 131
    and Queen Esther, 140–49

    and Ruth, 161–67
    sharing visibly, 112
    See also Mission statement
Mission field, getting facts on,
    105
Mission Partner, 27
Missions book, 69
Mission statement
    of author, 222–23
    benefit of, ix–x
    broadening, xiv, xvi–xvii
    checking, 65
    combining, with vision
        statement, 79–80
    communicating, 4
    covering both work and
        personal life, 65–68
    and creative tension zone,
        98
    defined, x, xi–xii
    difficulty of writing, xiv–xv
        elements of good, 3–7
    false assumptions about,
        9–22
    and goals, 105–6
    as harness and sword,
        xvii–xviii
    how to create, 50–65
    importance of having,
        ix–xi

importance of simplicity in, xvi, 5–6

length of, 3–4

matching employer's, 68–69

new process for creating, xv–xvi

as perfect fit, 25–31

problems from not having, xii–xiii

recited by memory, 4–6

unsuccessful or inadequate, 69–70

and work, 65–68

Money-making, 95–97

Moore, Terry, 43

Mordecai, 141, 142–43, 147, 148

Moses, 105, 155–61

  and accusations of others, 173, 174–75

  and fear, 183

  finding echoes of, 205–7

  and impatience, 184

  and small-mindedness of others, 176, 177

  and speech impediment, 171

  questions about, 161

Mother Teresa, 4

"My Job is my mission" assumption, 9–10

"My mission has to be a grand one or help a lot of people" assumption, 14

"My mission must be the same as those of my peers" assumption, 16–17

"My role is my mission" assumption, 10–11

"My 'To Do' list is my mission" assumption, 11–12

Naomi, 162–63, 165

Nebuchadnezzar, King, 195–96

Negative predictions

  exercise, 41

  using, as spur, 39–40

Nehemiah, 4, 105, 115–31

  and distraction, 179

  and fear, 183

  finding echoes of, 197–99

  questions about, 128–31

  and small-mindedness of others, 176, 177–78, 180–81

Numbers, 175

Obed, 165
O'Keefe, Georgia, 17–18
"One person only" mission
    statements, 70
Orpah, 162
Ortega, Ben, 44–45

Parallel job, 18–19
Parenting, 14
Parents' unlived lives, 34–38
    exercise, 37–38
Passion, 49–50
    exercise to find, 49–50
Past, 33–38, 170
Past Personality Influence
    (PPI), 33, 35
Peers, 16–17
People, as resources, 106
Personality
    exercises for knowing, 27–32
    and past, 33–38
    perfectly fitting mission to,
        25–27
Personal life, and mission
    statement, 65–68
Peter, 58
Pitfalls, 169–209
    accusations of others,
        173–76

apathy, 189–92
of champions, 196–97
compromise, 186–89
distraction, 179–81
and Esther, 203–4
fear, 181–83
feelings of inadequacy,
    170–73
impatience, 184–86
and Joan of Arc, 199–201
and Joseph, 201–3
and Moses, 205–7
and Nehemiah, 197–99
pride, 192–96
and Ruth, 208–9
small-mindedness of others,
    176–78
Point of power, 78–80
Politicians, 130
Positive prophecy
    chosen reaction to, 40
    exercise, 40–41
    power of, 38–41
    and vision statement,
        79
Potiphar, 150–51
Prayer, 112–14, 128, 136, 139,
    145, 148, 159, 166
Pride, 192–96
    questions about, 196

Princess Cariboo (film)
   and conscious creating,
      80–81
Purim, 147
Putting First Things First
   (Covey), x, 12

Recruiting, 86–88
Reengineering the Corporation
   (Hammer and
   Champy), x, 77
Reflection, 23
Relationships, 81–86
Relatives, 33
Religious leaders, 130
Repacking Your Bags (Leider
   and Shapiro), x
Reporters, 130
Resources, 106–8
   creating list of, 107–8
Retirement, 10
Revere, Paul, 14
Role, as mission, 10–11
Roosevelt, Franklin D.,
   3
Ruth, 161–67
   finding echoes of,
      208–9
   questions about, 167

Sacrifice, 16
Salk, Jonas, 213
Samuel, 171, 185
Samuel, 174, 195
Sanballat the Horonite, 118,
   119, 120, 180
"Saturate everything you do
   with prayer" step,
   112–14
   and Joan of Arc, 136,
      139
   and Moses, 159
   and Nehemiah, 128
   and Queen Esther, 145,
      148
   and Ruth, 166
Saul, King of Israel, 171
   and impatience, 184, 185
Self-esteem, xiii
Self-knowledge, 25–31, 33–47
   exercises, 27–30, 37–38,
      40–41, 43–44, 46–47
   and past, 33–38
   and positive prophecy,
      38–41
   and recognizing gifts,
      44–47
   and USP, 41–44
Self-serving interest (SSI),
   136

Sennacherib, King of Assyria, 187

Shapiro, David, x

Shebnah, 188

Shur, Barbara, 33

Simon Wiesenthal Museum, 13–14

60 Minutes (TV program), xii–xiii

Small-mindedness of others, 176–78

    questions about, 178

Solomon, King, 179–80, 190, 192

Song of Solomon, 192, 223

Speaking, 170

Specifics, importance of, 75, 80

Spence, Gerry, 87–88

State of the World Forum, 14

Stowe, Harriet Beecher, 14

Stress, 98

Suffering, 15–16

Sufi, 24

"Sustaining Structural Tension," 94–105

Talents, 106, 107

    reawakened," 109

Tangible things, 109–10

Teaching, 14

Teasdale, Sara, 13

"Technologies for Creating" workshop, 95

Territory of responsibility, 66

Thich Nhat Hanh, monk, 24

Tide detergent, and USP, 41

Time, 106, 107

Timing, 140–41

Tobiah the Ammonite, 118, 119, 120, 124, 180

"To-do" list, as mission, 11–12

Training, 106, 107

Trite or ordinary mission statements, 70

"Turn old business into new business" step, 108–9

    and Joan of Arc, 134

    and Moses, 159

    and Nehemiah, 126–27

    and Queen Esther, 145–46, 147

"Two Tramps in Mud Time" (Frost), 25

Uncle Tom's Cabin (Stowe), 14

Unemployment, xii, 26

Uninspiring mission state-
    ments, 69–70
Unintelligible mission state-
    ments, 70
Unique Selling Point (USP),
    41–44
    exercise, 43–44
USA Today, 26–27
Uzziah, King, 172
Uzziel, 120

Verb list, 50–58
Vision statement, 71–92
    combining with mission
        statement, 79–80
    creating, for relationships,
        81–86
    and creative tension, 93
    defined, 71–72
    exercise for companies,
        groups or associations,
        90–92
    exercise for individual,
        88–90
    and goals, 105–6
        key elements of, 73–74
    making real, through cre-
        ative tension, 94–100
    and Moses, 160

and point of power, 78–79
projection exercise, 77
as recruiting tool, 86–88
Spring in the Temple,
    223–25

Weapon, keeping one hand
    on, 130
What Could Be (WCB), 94
What Currently Is (WCI), 94
"What I am doing is as close as
    I can get to my real mis-
    sion" assumption, 18–19
Whyte, David, 15
Women
    Joan of Arc, 131–40
    Queen Esther, 105,
        140–49, 182, 203–4
    and "role as mission"
        assumption, 10–11
    Ruth, 161–67, 208–9
    and "wrongsizing," xiii–xiv
Word picture exercise, 29–30
Wordsworth, William, 42
"Wrongsizing" of America,
    xiii–xiv

Zipporah, 156

About the Author

Laurie Beth Jones has written multiple national best-selling books, including *Jesus, CEO: Using Ancient Wisdom for Visionary Leadership*; *Jesus in Blue Jeans: A Practical Guide to Everyday Spirituality*; and *The Path: Creating Your Mission Statement for Work and For Life*.

After launching and running her own successful advertising agency for fifteen years, Laurie Beth Jones burst onto the national scene with *Jesus, CEO*, a book that espoused bringing spiritual principles back into the business world. That book, and those that followed, spent more than thirteen months on the *Business Week* bestseller list, and have translated into twelve foreign languages, with worldwide sales nearing one million copies.

Using practical wisdom, humor, and reality-based thinking, Ms. Jones has become one of the world's leading consultants for businesses that want to take their work and their workers to unparalleled levels of performance, satisfaction, and success.

Her work has reached as high as the White House, the Pentagon, the halls of Congress and the Senate, as well as the depths of workers in the streets of Calcutta, Bosnia, and South Africa. She has been called upon by billionaires and kings to help discern their spiritual path, and lives out her mission, which is to "recognize, promote, and inspire the divine connection in myself and others."

She is a member of the Women's Action Council for Amnesty International, a sustaining contributor to World Vision International, and is currently helping build an orphanage outside of Juarez, Mexico, through her Jesus, CEO Foundation. She firmly believes that living out one's spiritual calling is the only path to joy, and that heaven will consist of all people fully expressing their highest gifts. She also believes that the business world is one of the most exciting arenas where this development can happen.

NATIONAL BESTSELLING TITLES
from LAURIE BETH JONES

JESUS, CEO

USING ANCIENT WISDOM FOR VISIONARY LEADERSHIP

In *Jesus, CEO*, national bestselling author Laurie Beth Jones creates an ingenious plan to heighten awareness and assist you in the process of mastering three categories of strength behind Jesus' leadership techniques — the strength of self-mastery, action, and relationships.

0-7868-8126-7 • $12.95 (pb)

JESUS IN BLUE JEANS

A PRACTICAL GUIDE TO EVERYDAY SPIRITUALITY

In *Jesus in Blue Jeans*, Laurie Beth Jones turns from the business world to everyday existence and reveals numerous ways of attaining spirituality and grace in our personal lives through the teachings of Jesus.

0-7868-8355-3 • $12.95 (pb)

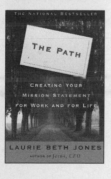

THE PATH

CREATING YOUR MISSION STATEMENT FOR WORK AND FOR LIFE

Offering inspiring and practical advice, Laurie Beth Jones leads readers through every step of both defining and fulfilling a mission. With more than ten years' experience in assisting groups and individuals, Jones provides clear, step-by-step guidance that can make writing a mission statement take a matter of hours rather than months or years.

0-7868-8241-7 • $11.95 (pb)

WWW.HYPERIONBOOKS.COM

HYPERION